COLORADO'S
QUIET
WINTER
TRAILS

COLORADO'S
QUIET
WINTER
TRAILS

DAVE MULLER

The Colorado Mountain Club Press
Golden, Colorado

Colorado's Quiet Winter Trails

PUBLISHED BY
The Colorado Mountain Club Press.

 Founded in 1912, The Colorado Mountain Club is the largest outdoor recreation, education and, conservation organization in the Rocky Mountains. Look for our books at your local bookstore or outdoor retailer or contact us at:

710 Tenth Street, #200, Golden, Colorado 80401

303-279-3080, ext. 2

Email: cmcpress@cmc.org

Alan Bernhard—design and composition
Mara Gaiser Chance—copy editor
Anna-Maria Crum—map maker
David Hite—photo editor
Alan Stark—publisher

DISTRIBUTED TO THE BOOK TRADE BY
Mountaineers Books

1001 SW Klickitat Way, Suite 201, Seattle, WA 98134, 800-553-4453

COVER IMAGE: Terry Root

 We gratefully acknowledge the financial support of the people of Colorado through the Scientific and Cultural Facilities District of greater metropolitan Denver for our publishing activities.

Reprinted 2021

ISBN 10: 0-9760525-1-2
ISBN 13: 978-0-9760525-1-7

Printed in the United States of America

ACKNOWLEDGMENTS

Because every human being on the planet is connected, I could legitimately thank a huge list of allies. To be more specific, however, I am especially grateful to my friend and mountain companion, D.J. Inman, whose great sensitivity to the negative impact of snowmobiles on certain backcountry trails led to the idea of this book. Many others accompanied me on these quiet trails. These include my wonderful wife, Jackie; my children, Tom, Andrew, Mary, Sara and Matthew; and their spouses and children, Frank Beghtel, Chris Belle, Tony Bianchi, Diane Gimber, Jane and Ken Fox, Liz and Kent Kreider, Jim Mahoney and Berneice Ybarra. Many other companions were willing to get an early start and brave the traffic and the elements. The Colorado Mountain Club, Alan Stark, and photographers David Hite, Terry Root, Dave Cooper and Jay Fell, and my office manager, Mairi Clark, have brought this book into production. I am grateful for the spectacular mountains of Colorado, the governmental agencies that serve and preserve them, and the Universe, God, the Source, which brought them and us into being.

COLORADO'S QUIET WINTER TRAILS

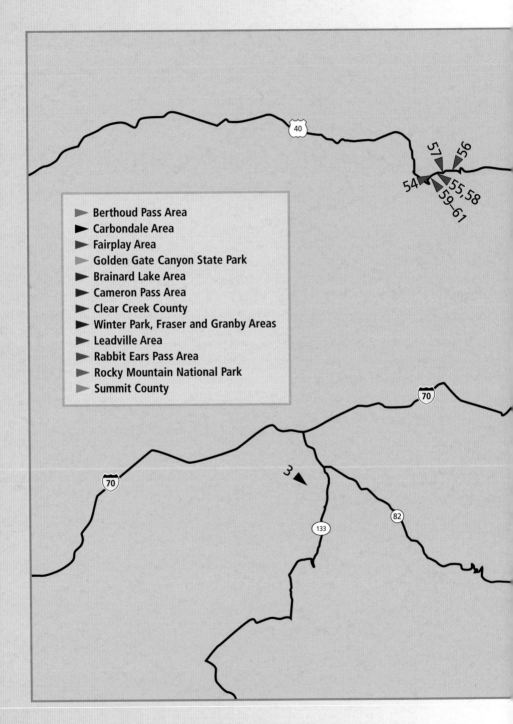

► Berthoud Pass Area
► Carbondale Area
► Fairplay Area
► Golden Gate Canyon State Park
► Brainard Lake Area
► Cameron Pass Area
► Clear Creek County
► Winter Park, Fraser and Granby Areas
► Leadville Area
► Rabbit Ears Pass Area
► Rocky Mountain National Park
► Summit County

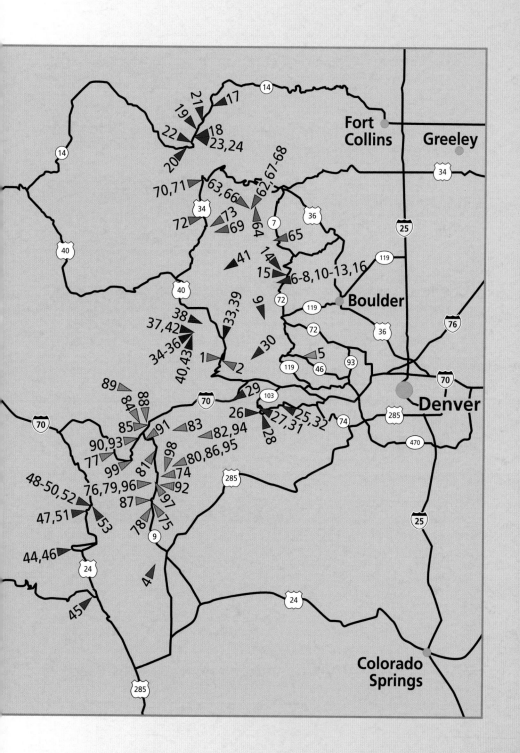

Contents

WINTER PARK, FRASER AND GRANBY AREAS

LEADVILLE AREA

RABBIT EARS PASS AREA

ROCKY MOUNTAIN NATIONAL PARK – EASTERN

ROCKY MOUNTAIN NATIONAL PARK – WESTERN

SUMMIT COUNTY

SIDEBARS

Introduction

The purpose of this book is to describe Colorado winter trails that can be enjoyed predominantly by snowshoers and cross-country skiers. Snowmobiles on the same track diminish the pleasure of the outdoor experience for many snowshoers and cross-country skiers. The noise, gas fumes, and the negative impact on the trail can be unpleasant. Even their speed can be troublesome as they pass too close. Of course, other noises may intrude on these trails, such as nearby downhill skiers, traffic on adjacent highways, overflying aircraft, or even snowmobiles far away.

The trails in this book should be free of private snowmobiles, but at times individuals may take their snowmobiles where they are not allowed. Occasionally, the organizations that administer these trails may use snowmobiles on these routes for maintenance or routine patrol reasons.

Nordic center trails have not been included because they generally offer less of the backcountry experience. These nordic centers, however, are great outdoor resources where equipment rentals, lessons, a warming house, and groomed trails can facilitate winter recreation.

Snowmobiles can be a wonderful means of transporting young and old alike into the lovely winter countryside. The author believes, however, that there is enough public land in Colorado to separate snowshoe and cross-country ski trails from snowmobile routes most of the time.

TRAILS: Every tour in this book uses a trail. Bushwacking is never necessary. Snowshoers are urged to travel outside of ski tracks whenever possible.

TIMES: These numbers are those of the author and should be considered a reference rather than a standard. Tour times will vary depending on snow conditions, air temperature, and other factors. Unless noted otherwise, most of the times given are for a cross-country skier.

ELEVATION GAIN: In most mountain treks, the trail often dips down at intervals on the way to the high point of the outing. Similarly, on the descent there are times when the trail rises. It is these extra feet of elevation gain which are included in the total elevation gain for each tour.

DIFFICULTY: The three categories of easiest, more difficult, and most difficult are used. These represent the opinion of the author. Very often the level of difficulty for the skier will be greater than for the snowshoer.

This is due to the greater difficulty for the skier in steep ascents and greater technical demands on steeper descents.

AVALANCHE DANGER: The least danger is present when the terrain is gradually sloped and usually tree-covered. Moderate danger is present with exposed, steeper slopes. No severe avalanche danger is present for any tour in this book. A recent heavy snowfall, wind and thawing temperatures will be factors in avalanche occurrences. When crossing potential avalanche chutes, it is advisable to spread a touring group into a well-spaced single file.

MAPS: A variety of maps are listed ranging from the most detailed 7.5 minute maps to the more general National Forest maps. This provides choices. Usually the Trails Illustrated map is best. If possible have a map and compass or GPS with you on these tours.

TEN ESSENTIALS: Throughout the book we note the Ten Essentials that you should have when in the backcountry. These Ten Essential Systems originated with The Mountaineers and are:

1. Navigation (map and compass)
2. Sun protection
3. Insulation (extra clothing)
4. Illumination (flashlight/headlamp)
5. First-aid supplies
6. Fire
7. Repair kit and tools
8. Nutrition (extra food)
9. Hydration (extra water)
10. Emergency shelter

The author has used all the trails in this book and hopes that these descriptions will enhance the Colorado winter mountain experience for many. It is the responsibility of the winter trekker on the trails to take adequate food and water, carry a compass and map, have the proper clothing and equipment, be aware of weather conditions, and use good judgment. The Colorado mountains can be especially dangerous in the winter. It is very easy to become lost.

1. First Creek Cabin

TOUR DISTANCE	0.8 mile each way
TOUR TIME	Up in 32 minutes, down in 26 minutes
STARTING ELEVATION	10,440 feet
HIGHEST ELEVATION	10,920 feet
ELEVATION GAIN	584 feet (includes 52 extra feet each way)
DIFFICULTY	More difficult
AVALANCHE DANGER	Least
RELEVANT MAPS	Trails Illustrated Number 103 Berthoud Pass 7.5 minute Grand County Number Four Arapaho National Forest

GETTING THERE: Drive 3.5 miles north of Berthoud Pass on U.S. 40. Park in the open area on the west side of the highway.

COMMENT: The First Creek Cabin is managed by The Colorado Mountain Club and can be rented for overnight use. The trail is a short but steep, winding ascent. Snowshoes are the preferred footwear for this outing. Cross-country skiers must be expert to try this and will generally require climbing skins. This trail is described as a ski tour in other guidebooks. If you stay on the proper trail and remain on the east side of the major creek drainage, there is no avalanche danger. Higher to the west of the trail and cabin, the avalanche danger increases. Therefore, stay on the trail.

THE TOUR: Start out to the northwest and follow the curling trail through the forest up to a fork at the halfway point. Continue upward on the right fork as the trail gets steeper. Soon the trail curves to the right and becomes somewhat more gradual as it switchbacks up over a ridge before reaching First Creek Cabin. A plaque honors Christina J. Hahn and Robert J. Belter, who lost their lives in separate avalanches nine years apart. If renters are in the cabin, keep your distance and don't disturb them. From the cabin you can see a few peaks through the trees. Colorado Mines Peak is southeast. An unnamed peak (elevation 11,527 feet) is west southwest and the Twin Cones are west northwest. After your break at the cabin, return steeply on your ascent route.

Colorado Mountain Club members D.J. Inman and Tony Bianchi at First Creek Cabin. PHOTO BY DAVE MULLER

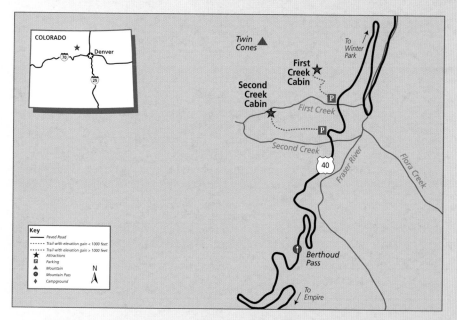

2. Second Creek

TOUR DISTANCE	1.2 miles each way
TOUR TIME	Up in 60 minutes, down in 45 minutes
STARTING ELEVATION	10,595 feet
HIGHEST ELEVATION	11,350 feet
ELEVATION GAIN	815 feet (includes 30 extra feet each way)
DIFFICULTY	More difficult
AVALANCHE DANGER	Moderate
RELEVANT MAPS	Trails Illustrated Number 103 Berthoud Pass 7.5 minute Grand County Number Four Arapaho National Forest

GETTING THERE: From Berthoud Pass, drive north on U.S. 40 for 2.9 miles. Park on the left in an open area at some trail signs and a curve in the road.

COMMENT: Berthoud Pass connects Clear Creek and Grand Counties and is located on the Continental Divide. The pass is named for Captain Edward L. Berthoud, a Swiss, who was the chief engineer of the Colorado Central Railroad in the late 1800s. Descending north from Berthoud Pass, the first three drainages into the Fraser River are Current Creek, Second Creek, and First Creek. The most suitable of these for cross-country skiing is Second Creek. The tour up the Second Creek drainage is quite steep until you reach the higher parts of the basin. There you find many opportunities for a more gradual ascent. Due to its proximity to the Front Range and its short distance, the Second Creek tour is possible for a half-day outing. I recommend this trek for a good workout during the first half of the season and when snow conditions are favorable.

THE TOUR: Begin up and west from the parking area. There are usually many different tracks ascending this basin. Generally keep to the right (north). Proceed west through the trees and you will encounter a series of three benches or terraces. On top of the second such bench, just west of a rocky buttress, you will find a picnic table and a small hut, which is closed to the public. This structure was once called the Gwen Andrews Hut and is the arbitrary terminus of this tour. Much free skiing and snowshoeing is available above and past the third bench. From the hut, James Peak and Parry Peak can be seen to the northeast. Colorado Mines Peak lies to the southeast. The descent is rapid for the skier and requires intermediate skills at least. The greatest avalanche danger lies to the south, so stay north of Second Creek.

A sunny day in the trees near Berthoud Pass.

PHOTO BY JAY FELL

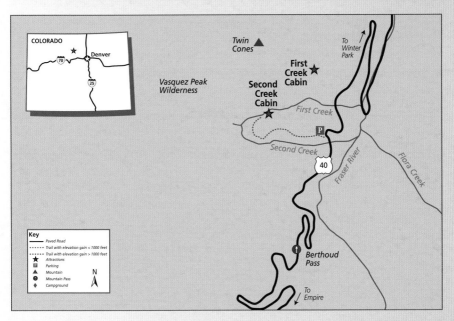

17

3. Paul's Point (Spring Gulch Trail System)

TOUR DISTANCE	2 miles each way
TOUR TIME	Up in 54 minutes, down in 37 minutes
STARTING ELEVATION	7,760 feet
HIGHEST ELEVATION	8,300 feet
ELEVATION GAIN	690 feet (includes 75 extra feet each way)
DIFFICULTY	More difficult
AVALANCHE DANGER	Least
RELEVANT MAPS	Trails Illustrated Number 143 Spring Gulch Trail System Map Stony Ridge 7.5 minute Pitkin County Number One White River National Forest

GETTING THERE: From Colorado 82 south of Glenwood Springs, turn west into Carbondale on Colorado 133. After 1 mile, turn right at the traffic light onto Road 108. Follow this main road, which becomes the Thompson Creek Road for 6.8 miles, and turn right into the parking area on the right at the trailhead for the Spring Gulch Trail System.

COMMENT: The Spring Gulch Trail System of cross-country ski trails is located southwest of Carbondale and offers 12 miles of groomed trails. No fee is required but memberships and donations are encouraged. Dogs, sleds, snowboards, and vehicles are forbidden. The shortest route to Paul's Point will be described. This involves a steady uphill ski through bushes and small trees, with some great views of Mount Sopris along the way. Paul's Point is an overlook that honors Paul Lappala, one of the founders of this winter trail system, who died in 1993. There are, of course, many other trails in this system that can be explored.

THE TOUR: Begin to the left of the information board and gently ascend to the south on the Lazy Eight Trail. After 150 yards, take the left fork. You will encounter a series of well-marked intersections along the way. Use the map of the trails that is available at the trailhead. From Lazy Eight, take the Roundabout Trail to the left and then Wagon Road and Sidewinder upward to Finlandia. Turn left upon reaching Finlandia. You will reach a terminal loop at Paul's Point within 50 yards. A sign identifies several of the mountains that can be seen from here. Mount Sopris is closest and the most impressive to the east southeast. Capitol Peak and Snowmass Peak lie to the southeast, and Hawk Peak is to the south southeast. If you return by your ascent route, there are many good runs to enjoy.

The author on the Spring Gulch Trail System with Mount Sopris in the background.

PHOTO BY JACKIE MULLER

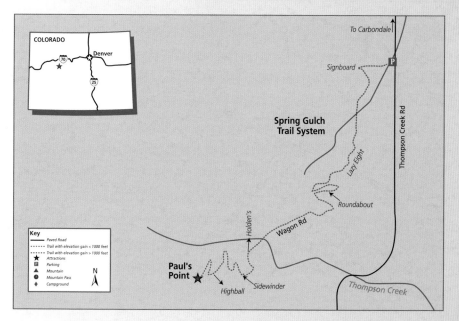

4. Tie Hack Loop

TOUR DISTANCE	5.5 miles (total loop)
TOUR TIME	Up to loop in 26 minutes, loop in 98 minutes, and down from loop in 14 minutes (total time 138 minutes)
STARTING ELEVATION	10,040 feet
HIGHEST ELEVATION	10,750 feet
ELEVATION GAIN	1,140 feet. (includes 430 extra feet)
DIFFICULTY	More difficult
AVALANCHE DANGER	Least
RELEVANT MAPS	Trails Illustrated Number 110 Fairplay West 7.5 minute Park County Number One Pike National Forest

GETTING THERE: From the junction of U.S. 285 and Colorado 9, southeast of Fairplay, drive south on U.S. 285 for 1.2 miles and turn right onto the Fourmile Creek Road, which is County Road 18. After 1.2 miles on this good, wide road keep left at the fork. At 3.4 miles from U.S. 285, park on the right at the road and trail sign.

COMMENT: This loop can be traveled in either direction and proceeds through the forest on mostly a narrow trail. A "tie hack" was a worker who shaped ties for train tracks in the early days of the railroads.

THE TOUR: Start west northwest up the road. If the snow is inadequate, carry your gear a few hundred yards. The snow will be better higher on the road in the trees. Quickly connect with the blue diamond markers on the trees and follow these carefully. They will mark your entire route. Proceed generally west northwest and continue straight at an unmarked four-way intersection. At 1 mile from the trailhead, you reach some signs and the beginning of the loop. The clockwise route will be described. Ascend to the left (west southwest), over steeper terrain and reach a sign pointing to Sheep Mountain after 0.5 mile on the loop. Another 0.4 mile brings you to a clearing and a fork. Find the blue marker and continue to your right (north) and back into the trees for another mile before connecting with an old mining road. Again you proceed to the right (north) and descend to an intersection with a "Fuelwood Area" sign on the left. Turn right here and quickly leave the road and follow the blue markers through the forest. Continue 1.6 miles from the last fork through some open areas to return to the beginning of the loop. It is an easy glide for the skier down the left (southeast) fork back to your vehicle.

Trailheaad, Tie Hack Loop.

PHOTO BY DAVE MULLER

PHOTO BY DAVID HITE

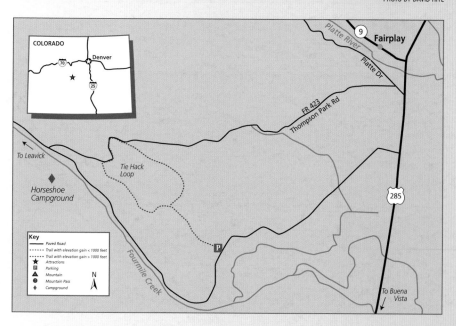

5. Frazer Meadow

TOUR DISTANCE	2.3 miles each way
TOUR TIME	Out in 70 minutes, back in 58 minutes (snowshoer's times)
STARTING ELEVATION	8,400 feet
HIGHEST ELEVATION	9,200 feet
ELEVATION GAIN	1,260 feet (includes 460 extra feet)
DIFFICULTY	More difficult
AVALANCHE DANGER	Least
RELEVANT MAPS	Trails Illustrated Number 100 Golden Gate Canyon State Park (available at the visitor center) Black Hawk 7.5 minute Gilpin County

GETTING THERE: From Colorado 93 northwest of Golden, drive west on Jefferson County Road 70 for 12.6 miles (keep left at mile 3.8). At the intersection with the visitor center on the right, go left and drive for less than 2 miles to the Mountain Base Road on the right. Go right here and quickly take another right fork and ascend 0.2 mile to the Kriley Pond Overlook parking area and trailhead. A trail fee is required.

COMMENT: When there is ample snow, Golden Gate Canyon State Park can provide some good winter tours. One of these begins above Kriley Pond, rises to a ridge, and continues down to the cabin ruins in Frazer Meadow. Because the Mountain Base Road may not be plowed, this starting point at the Kriley Pond Overlook Trail is recommended. Snowshoers will have an easier time on this trek, as skiers will be challenged by the narrow, often winding trail.

THE TOUR: Begin north past an outhouse on the well-marked Blue Grouse Trail. Ascend 0.7 mile to a junction with the Mule Deer Trail. Go right (northeast) and continue your ascent to a high point on a ridge. Stay on the Mule Deer Trail and avoid the several side trails. The old cabins in Frazer Meadow, at a four-way inter-section, make a fine destination. Refresh, renew, and enjoy this lovely meadow before returning southwest on your outbound route.

SIDEBAR: WHEN IT DUMPS ON THE FLATLANDS

The focus of this book is quiet winter trails — that is, trails where snowmobiles are not allowed — but there are some very fine places to ski without snowmobiles when we get a big snowstorm in the Flatlands. Our favorites are the large city parks where you will find that the early bird track skiers and skaters have already broken trail and maybe even packed down the snow.

Ken Fox, Tony Bianchi, and D.J. Inman at Frazer Meadow.

PHOTO BY DAVE MULLER

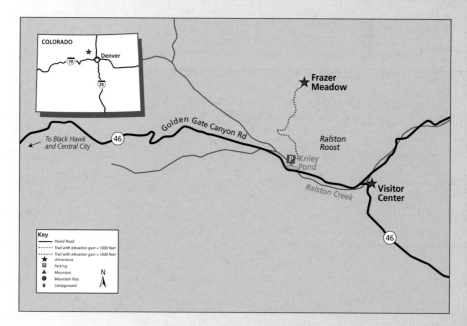

6. CMC – Brainard Lake Road Loop

TOUR DISTANCE	5.2 miles (total loop)
TOUR TIME	Out in 90 minutes, back in 62 minutes
STARTING ELEVATION	10,080 feet
HIGHEST ELEVATION	10,400 feet
ELEVATION GAIN	825 feet (includes 505 extra feet)
DIFFICULTY	More difficult
AVALANCHE DANGER	Least
RELEVANT MAPS	Trails Illustrated Number 102 Ward 7.5 minute Boulder County Roosevelt National Forest

GETTING THERE: Drive north from Nederland, west of Boulder, on Colorado 72 for 11.7 miles. Turn left onto the Brainard Lake Road and continue for 2.7 miles. Park on the right at the Red Rock Trailhead just before a road barrier. A fee is often charged at the trailhead. Regular cars can reach the trailhead unless snow and ice have not been plowed.

COMMENT: When the snow is ample and the winds are calm, the lovely Brainard Lake area offers many well-marked trails for the nordic skier and snowshoer. This loop takes you through the forest in a clockwise direction to Brainard Lake with a return on the wide Brainard Lake Road. This Indian Peaks area is very popular in both winter and summer.

THE TOUR: Begin south on foot up the road leading to the Left Hand Reservoir. After a steep 0.5 mile, take the right fork at a sign and enter the trees on the Colorado Mountain Club South Trail (CMC South). Follow the signs and blue diamond tree markers for at least 2 miles to a pair of old chimneys and a signed trail fork. The Little Raven Trail leads to the left. Continue straight another 150 yards down to the Brainard Lake Road. Then ascend to the right with Brainard Lake on your left and follow this wide road back down to your original starting point. The total loop is more than 5 miles.

Self portrait of John and Kris Wallack near Brainard Lake.

PHOTO BY JOHN WALLACK

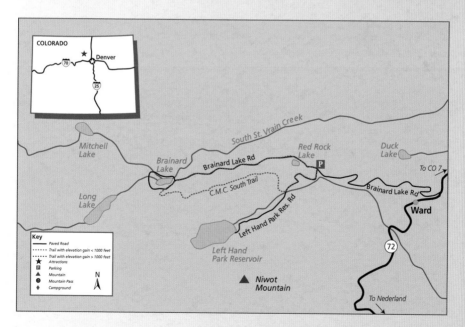

25

7. CMC Cabin via Waldrop Trail

TOUR DISTANCE	Out in 2.8 miles, back in 3 miles
TOUR TIME	Out in 97 minutes, back in 50 minutes
STARTING ELEVATION	10,080 feet
HIGHEST ELEVATION	10,400 feet
ELEVATION GAIN	570 feet (includes 250 extra feet)
DIFFICULTY	Most difficult
AVALANCHE DANGER	Least
RELEVANT MAPS	Trails Illustrated Number 102 Ward 7.5 minute Boulder County Roosevelt National Forest

GETTING THERE: From Nederland, drive north on Colorado 72 for 11.7 miles and turn left on the Brainard Lake Road. After 2.7 miles on this paved road, park at the Red Rock Trailhead just before reaching a road barrier.

COMMENT: Another good winter destination for the nordic skier and snowshoer in the Brainard Lake area is the CMC Brainard Cabin, built in 1928. The cabin serves as a weekend warming hut and can be rented for overnight use. There are several well-marked routes to the cabin. The Waldrop Trail, with its occasional steep sections, connects with the South Saint Vrain Trail before reaching a side trail to the cabin.

THE TOUR: Begin the tour west from the winter closure gate. Follow the Brainard Lake Road for 200 yards to a sign for the Waldrop Trail on the right. Exit the road and enter the trees to the north on the Waldrop Trail, which curls through pine forest with periodic blue diamond tree blazes to reach a signed fork in the middle of a meadow, at 1.5 miles of the tour. Continue straight to a crossing of South Saint Vrain Creek and a junction with South Saint Vrain Trail at more directional signs. Go left (southwest) here, 0.25 mile, to another signed fork. The left fork is the Brainard Cutoff Trail and leads back to Brainard Lake in another 0.5 mile. You, however, take the right fork and stay on the South Saint Vrain Trail another 0.25 mile to yet another sign at a trail junction. Go left here and follow the blue diamond tree blazes to the CMC Brainard Cabin. After some respite at the cabin, which is often open on the weekends, continue west 75 yards to a wide road, which leads to the Mitchell Lake Trailhead on the right. Descend to the left, however, and take a series of left forks that lead you past Brainard Lake on the right and then through campsites to the Brainard Lake Road back down to your starting point.

Tony Bianchi at the Colorado Mountain Club cabin near Brainard Lake.

PHOTO BY DAVE MULLER

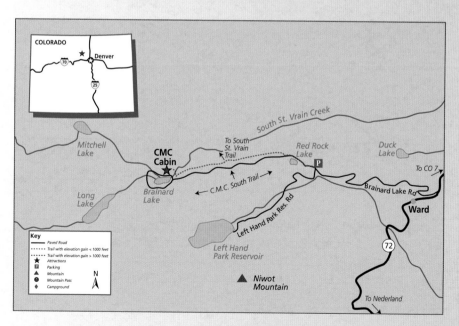

27

8. CMC South Trail

TOUR DISTANCE	2.8 miles each way
TOUR TIME	Out in 58 minutes, back in 48 minutes
STARTING ELEVATION	10,080 feet
HIGHEST ELEVATION	10,390 feet
ELEVATION GAIN	640 feet (includes 330 extra feet)
DIFFICULTY	More difficult
AVALANCHE DANGER	Least
RELEVANT MAPS	Trails Illustrated Number 102 Ward 7.5 minute Boulder County Roosevelt National Forest

GETTING THERE: From Nederland, drive north on Colorado 72 for 11.8 miles and turn left onto the Brainard Lake Road. Follow this plowed road for 2.6 miles and park on the right near the Red Rock Trailhead signboard just before the metal roadblock. Regular cars can reach this area. A fee may be charged.

COMMENT: The Brainard Lake area near the Indian Peaks Wilderness offers many connecting trails for ski touring and snowshoeing. One of these is the Colorado Mountain Club (CMC) South Trail, which parallels the Brainard Lake Road. High winds often rake this area, resulting in variable snow conditions. Dogs are forbidden on the CMC South Trail, as well as some of the other trails in this area.

THE TOUR: Start on foot south up the road to Left Hand Park Reservoir. Pass a trail on the right just before the metal barrier. This will be your exit point on the CMC South Trail. After 0.3 mile up the wide road, take the right fork at a sign and descend northwest 75 yards into the trees to more signs and a trail intersection. Ascend the left fork toward Brainard Lake. Remember this junction for your return. Follow the narrow trail as it rises and falls through the woods. Be sure to follow the blue diamond markers on the trees, which define your route. At the halfway point, pass a sign and trail on your right. Continue straight to the southwest for the second half of your outward tour. The arbitrary turnaround point is the junction with the Little Raven Trail on the left. A sign and some chimney remnants mark this area. Brainard Lake lies below by trail to the right. (Ascending the Little Raven Trail on the left leads to a higher point on the Left Hand Park Reservoir Road.) For the return on the CMC South Trail, retrace your route back to the fork and signs near the trailhead. Go left instead of ascending the right fork to the Left Hand Road. Within another 60 yards, go right at another sign and take the easier way back along Brainard Lake Road to your original trailhead.

CMC members approach the turnaround point near the chimneys on the CMC South Trail. PHOTO BY JAY FELL

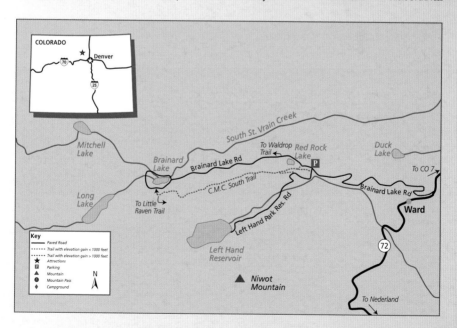

29

9. Eldora to King Lake Trailhead

TOUR DISTANCE	2.8 miles each way
TOUR TIME	Up in 81 minutes, down in 53 minutes
STARTING ELEVATION	8,820 feet
HIGHEST ELEVATION	9,625 feet
ELEVATION GAIN	1,005 feet (includes 200 extra feet)
DIFFICULTY	More difficult
AVALANCHE DANGER	Least
RELEVANT MAPS	Trails Illustrated Number 102 Nederland 7.5 minute Boulder County Roosevelt National Forest

GETTING THERE: From Nederland, west of Boulder, at the intersection of Colorado 119 and Colorado 72, drive south on Colorado 119 for 0.6 mile. Then turn right onto Boulder County Road 130 and set your mileage to zero. Keep right at mile 1.4 and continue through the town of Eldora to where the road plowing ends at 3.8 miles. Heed the signs and park legally.

COMMENT: The small town of Eldora, outside of Nederland, is the starting point for this tour into the lovely Indian Peaks Wilderness. Be sure there is ample snow before you take this tour because the route can be rocky. There are many other well-marked trails in the area that are not frequented by snowmobiles.

THE TOUR: Start out to the west and ascend the wide road up to a fork and signs after 1 mile. Descend the left fork (west northwest) as the right fork ascends to the Fourth of July Campground. Soon pass through the former site of the town Hessie, and shortly thereafter reach the summer Hessie Trailhead. Cross the North Fork of the Middle Boulder Creek and pass by an Indian Peaks Wilderness signboard. The road soon becomes steeper as you rise to a crossing of the South Fork of Middle Boulder Creek. Continue up to the Lost Creek Trail on the left. Pass it and persist to the west another 0.3 mile to another South Fork crossing and a signed trail fork. The left fork leads to King Lake, and the right fork continues to Woodland Lake, Skyscraper Reservoir, Jasper Lake, and Devils Thumb Lake. This fork is the turn-around point of this tour. Your return time will be shorter.

SIDEBAR: SOMETHING TO SIT ON

If you are surrounded by snow and you want to sit down, you'll need something to sit on in the snow. We carry a bivy bag, an essential piece of gear if there is any chance you might get caught out and have to hunker down. The bivy bag will seat two.

D.J. Inman and Frank Beghtel en route to the King Lake Trailhead.
PHOTO BY DAVE MULLER

Hessie trailhead sign.   PHOTO BY DAVID HITE

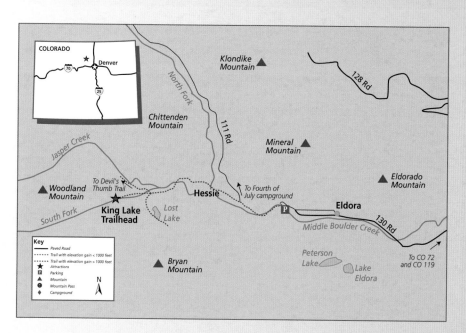

31

10. Left Hand Reservoir

TOUR DISTANCE	1.8 miles each way
TOUR TIME	Up in 60 minutes, down in 38 minutes
STARTING ELEVATION	10,075 feet
HIGHEST ELEVATION	10,620 feet
ELEVATION GAIN	675 feet (includes an extra 65 feet each way)
DIFFICULTY	More difficult
AVALANCHE DANGER	Least
RELEVANT MAPS	Trails Illustrated Number 102 Ward 7.5 minute Boulder County Roosevelt National Forest

GETTING THERE: Either drive south from Colorado 7 on Colorado 72 (the Peak to Peak Highway) for 11.8 miles or drive north from Nederland on Colorado 72 for 11.7 miles to the Brainard Lake Road on the west side of the highway. Then drive 2.6 miles up the Brainard Lake Road and park on the right near the trail signs.

COMMENT: Numerous winter trails originate from the Brainard Lake Road. This one is often windblown and ascends a wide and sometimes steep road to Left Hand Reservoir and a magnificent panorama of the Indian Peaks. The Little Raven Ski Trail makes several connections with the road to Left Hand Reservoir. Dogs are allowed on this trail but are forbidden on many of the other routes. The trailhead sign clarifies these prohibitions. Chief Left Hand was a name given to Niwot, a leader of the Southern Arapaho tribe of Native Americans.

THE TOUR: From the parking area, cross the road and begin your tour from the Red Rock Trailhead to the south. Follow this side road and pass trailhead signs and a road barrier. Ascend the winding main road through the evergreen forest. After 0.25 mile from the trailhead, avoid the CMC South Trail on the right and persist upward. At the 1 mile mark, cross a bridge over Lefthand Creek and climb steeply as the road curves left and then right. Avoid the Little Raven Ski Trail on the left at a sign. Continue generally southwest and pass another link of the Little Raven Trail, this time on the right, after another 0.5 mile. Stay on the gradually ascending road past a clearing on the left. You soon reach a sign just below Left Hand Reservoir. At the lip of this body of water, you can see many of the Indian Peaks, mostly to the west. Tracing a clockwise direction, there is Niwot Mountain to the south southeast; Navajo Peak, Apache Peak and Shoshoni Peak to the southwest; and Mount Toll, Paiute Peak, and Mount Audubon to the west northwest.

Along the Left Hand Reservoir Trail after a snow storm.

PHOTO BY DAVE MULLER

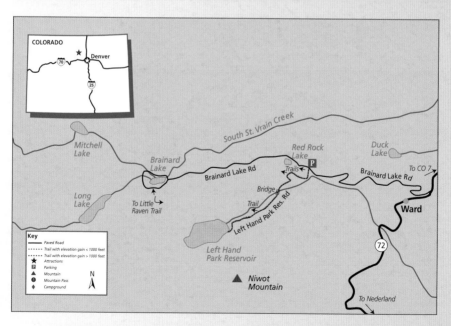

11. Little Raven – CMC Loop

TOUR DISTANCE	0.75 mile on Lefthand Reservoir Road, 2.25 miles on Little Raven Trail and 2.8 miles on the CMC trail for 5.8 total miles.
TOUR TIME	146 minutes (total loop)
STARTING ELEVATION	10,080 feet
HIGHEST ELEVATION	10,595 feet
ELEVATION GAIN	1,090 feet (includes 575 extra feet)
DIFFICULTY	More difficult
AVALANCHE DANGER	Least
RELEVANT MAPS	Trails Illustrated Number 102 Ward 7.5 minute Boulder County Roosevelt National Forest

GETTING THERE: Drive north from Nederland, west of Boulder, on Colorado 72 for 11.7 miles and turn left onto the Brainard Lake Road. Follow this plowed road for 2.7 miles and park on the right at the Red Rock Trailhead just before the metal road barrier. A fee may be charged.

COMMENT: Two of the many cross-country ski and snowshoe trails in the Brainard Lake area, east of the Indian Peaks Wilderness, are the Little Raven Trail and the CMC Trail. The Brainard Lake Area is often raked by high winds. Much of this loop tour, however, lies in the forest with more protection from wind gusts. Many blue tree blazes clearly mark these two trails. Dogs and snowmobiles are forbidden on this loop. A clockwise direction of the loop is described here.

THE TOUR: Begin on foot on the road leading south from the parking area. Pass around a road barrier and follow this road as it winds upward toward Left Hand Reservoir. Pass a side trail on the right, which leads to the CMC Trail, and continue on the road to a higher junction 0.75 mile from your starting point. At a sign, take the Little Raven Trail on the right and enter the woods to the southwest. The trail then rises and falls for the next 2.25 miles to a trail intersection, a sign, and an informational plaque about Chief Little Raven, a principal chief of the Southern Arapahoes in the late 1800s. You are just above Brainard Lake. The left fork continues down to the road. You continue the clockwise loop to the northeast (right) on the CMC Trail. Pass two chimney remnants and follow the serpentine trail past a side trail on the left for 2.8 miles back to the lower part of the Left Hand Reservoir Road near your parking area. The last few hundred yards of this loop separate into a snowshoe trail on the right and the nordic ski trail on the left.

TOP: Little Raven Trail off of Lefthand Reservoir Trail.   PHOTO BY DAVE MULLER

BOTTOM: The author and friends.   PHOTO BY JACKIE MULLER

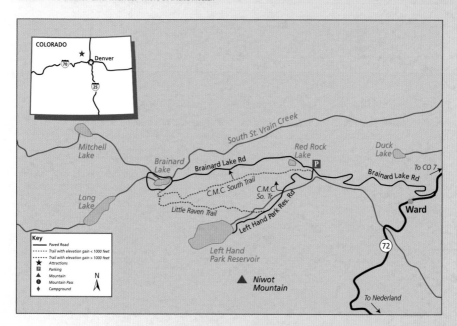

12. Long Lake

TOUR DISTANCE	2.6 miles for the Waldrop Trail, 1.9 miles to and from Long Lake, 2.8 miles for the CMC South Trail for a total of 7.3 miles.
TOUR TIME	Up in 122 minutes, down in 102 minutes
STARTING ELEVATION	10,080 feet
HIGHEST ELEVATION	10,541 feet (above Long Lake)
ELEVATION GAIN	1,661 feet (includes 1,200 extra feet)
DIFFICULTY	Most difficult
AVALANCHE DANGER	Least
RELEVANT MAPS	Trails Illustrated Number 102 Ward 7.5 minute Boulder County Roosevelt National Forest

GETTING THERE: See description for Little Raven – CMC Loop on page 34.

COMMENT: This loop requires fresh snow and is more demanding than the signs would indicate.

THE TOUR: Begin west on the road for about 100 yards past the metal barrier. Take the right fork onto the Waldrop Trail, following it as it meanders in a counterclockwise direction up the valley. After 1.5 miles, keep right (west northwest) as a side trail back to the Brainard Lake Road leads up to the left. At 0.4 mile from this fork, go left at a sign as the South Saint Vrain Trail enters from the right. After 0.1 mile, go right (west) at a sign and fork. Keep straight at the next sign at 0.4 mile. The trail then curves to the right (west) and joins a paved road leading to Mitchell and Blue Lakes Trailhead. Go left on the road and descend 100 yards before reaching the road to the Long Lake parking area. Go right (south) and ascend this road for 0.3 mile to the Long Lake Trailhead. Continue south southwest from here for 0.4 mile until you reach a point overlooking Long Lake, with some of the Indian Peaks to the southwest and west. To return, retrace your route back to the Long Lake parking area. Turn right here and descend to the road encircling Brainard Lake and go right. Quickly pass a picnic area on the left and then follow the tracks southeast off the road in the trees. Within 150 yards you will reach a monument to Chief Little Raven; take the left fork onto the CMC South Trail. (The right fork is the Little Raven Trail.) Soon you will pass two old chimneys and follow the blue diamond markers past a side trail on the left, which connects to the Brainard Lake Road. Continue to the parking area on the CMC South Trail. A final segment of this loop divides into a cross-country trail on the left and a snowshoe trail on the right.

A shack on the way to Long Lake.

PHOTO BY DAVE MULLER

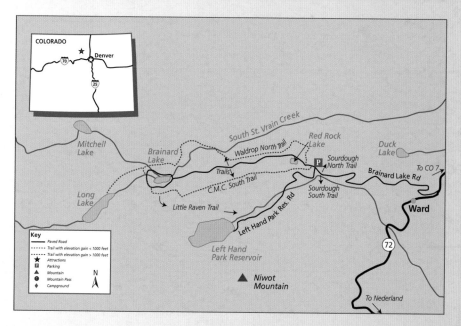

37

13. Middle Sourdough Trail

TOUR DISTANCE	6.5 miles (one way)
TOUR TIME	170 minutes
STARTING ELEVATION	10,050 feet
HIGHEST ELEVATION	10,130 feet
ELEVATION GAIN	1,130 feet (includes 1,050 extra feet)
DIFFICULTY	Most difficult
AVALANCHE DANGER	Least
RELEVANT MAPS	Trails Illustrated 102 Ward 7.5 minute Boulder County Roosevelt National Forest

GETTING THERE: See description for Little Raven – CMC Loop on page 34.

COMMENT: The best way to enjoy the Sourdough Trail is to start at the Red Rock Trailhead in the middle, ski down one way either north or south, and have a vehicle at a lower trailhead.

THE TOUR: Begin to the east northeast and follow the blue blazes for this entire tour. Descend 1 mile to the bridge crossing South Saint Vrain Creek and a signed trail fork just beyond the bridge. Take the left fork and ascend to the west. You are now on the combined Sourdough and South Saint Vrain Trails. After another 1.2 miles, you reach another trail sign at a fork. Ascend sharply and steeply to the right (north) for another 0.3 mile to a ridge. Then turn east and descend a tree-lined ravine, which curves left past an old Wapiti Trail sign. Soon you reach a level, semi-open area with a large clearing below on your right. Follow the blazes to a signed trail fork at 3 miles from the trailhead. Continue to the right (east southeast) another 0.3 mile to another sign and fork in the trees. Now go left (northeast) and continue past a large clearing to reach a solitary, wooden pole at an open ridge point. From here descend slightly before curving left and re-entering the trees. Pass an old Baptiste Trail sign on the right, and follow the descending trail to the left. At 4.4 miles there is an intersection and a sign as the Sourdough Trail makes a sharp left and then a right turn. Continue down the right fork 0.25 mile to another signed fork. Take the right fork designated Trail 850. At 5.4 miles you reach a clearing and signs as a summer road crosses the Sourdough Trail. Continue across the clearing and ascend a large open hill with many burnt tree stumps. Climb to a ridge, curve to the left, and descend through the old burn area to enter the trees once more. Turn left to reach the road and trailhead sign on the Beaver Reservoir Road.

North trailhead for Middle Sourdough Trail.

PHOTO BY DAVE MULLER

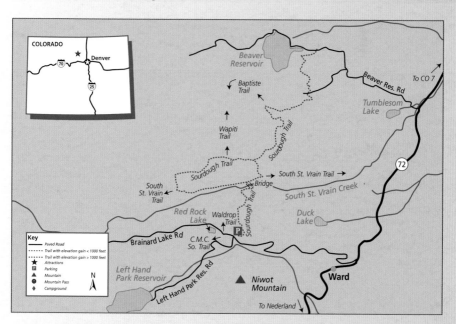

14. North Sourdough Trail

TOUR DISTANCE	2.2 miles each way
TOUR TIME	Out in 56 minutes, back in 80 minutes
STARTING ELEVATION	9,150 feet
HIGHEST ELEVATION	9,150 feet
LOWEST ELEVATION	8,560 feet
ELEVATION GAIN	766 feet (includes 88 feet each way)
DIFFICULTY	Most difficult
AVALANCHE DANGER	Least
RELEVANT MAPS	Trails Illustrated Number 102 Allens Park 7.5 minute Ward 7.5 minute Boulder County

GETTING THERE: From Nederland, drive north on Colorado 72 for 14.1 miles. Turn left onto Road 96, the Beaver Reservoir Road, for 1.9 miles and park off the road near the trail on the right.

COMMENT: The Sourdough Trail has three sections as it runs north to south for over 15 miles along the eastern flank of the Indian Peaks. The trail provides a group of classic ski tours and good snowshoe routes with plenty of steep ups and downs. Snowmobiles are forbidden on the entire Sourdough Trail. There are occasional views of the adjacent mountains, but most of these trails pass through the forest, which limits the vistas. Many other trails connect with the Sourdough. The area around Brainard Lake and the eastern slopes of the Indian Peaks is often windblown with irregular snow cover. The best times for this outing will be in the second half of the cross-country ski and snowshoe season, preferably after some recent snowfall. This northern segment is ideal for the snowshoer, but advanced skills are necessary for the nordic skier as the narrow trail has several steep and curving parts. Follow the blue diamond markers on the trees.

THE TOUR: Start off on the trail to the north and enter the forest. Soon you cross a boardwalk and arrive at a signed fork at the halfway point. Take the trail to the right (north) and continue through the woods another 0.4 mile to a second signed fork. Once again take the right fork to the north. Keep right at two more unmarked trail junctions as you generally proceed to the north northeast and reach Peaceful Valley at a sign for the Middle Saint Vrain Trail. The more difficult leg of this tour will be on the return as you retrace the route. Occasional glimpses of the Indian Peaks are available along the way.

Road leading to the north trailhead of the North Sourdough Trail.

PHOTO BY DAVE MULLER

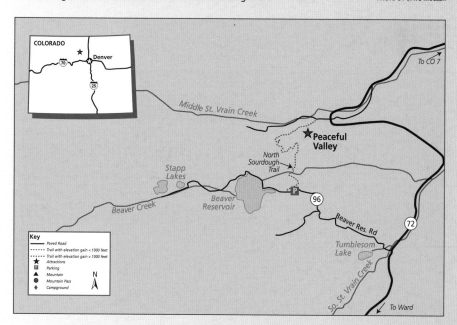

41

15. South Saint Vrain Trail

TOUR DISTANCE	3 miles each way
TOUR TIME	Up in 87 minutes, down in 59 minutes
STARTING ELEVATION	8,750 feet
HIGHEST ELEVATION	9,530 feet
ELEVATION GAIN	990 feet (includes 105 extra feet each way)
DIFFICULTY	Most difficult
AVALANCHE DANGER	Least
RELEVANT MAPS	Trails Illustrated Number 102 Gold Hill 7.5 minute Ward 7.5 minute Boulder County

GETTING THERE: From Nederland, drive north on Colorado 72 for 14 miles. Turn left on the Beaver Lake Road (Boulder County Road 96) for 50 yards, and park along the roadside. The South Saint Vrain Trailhead is on the left. Boulder County Road 96 lies 9.3 miles south of the intersection of Colorado 7 and Colorado 72.

COMMENT: The South Saint Vrain Trail is very steep in the first mile from the eastern trailhead. Then it becomes more gradual as it continues to the west. Unlike the Brainard Lake area, no entry fee is charged, and much of the frequent heavy winds in the Brainard Lake area are avoided due to the lower elevation. This is a good forest trek with many aspen trees and few vistas. Snowshoers will have the easiest time on the South Saint Vrain Trail. The narrow, twisting trail will tax the cross-country skier. Climbing skins are recommended for the initial third of this tour.

THE TOUR: Begin on foot to the south with the South Saint Vrain Creek on the left. Ascend steeply 1 mile before the terrain becomes level. Pass through several lovely meadows abounding in aspen. After 2.5 miles, pass around or over a road barrier and reach a fork shortly thereafter. Avoid the trail on the left, which connects to the Brainard Lake Road. Continue straight (southwest) for another 0.5 mile to an open gate at the Baptist Camp as the South Saint Vrain Trail turns north, leaves the road, and continues west to cross the Sourdough Trail. You have traveled 3 miles, and this is a good turnaround point for this outing.

SIDEBAR: GORP

It is more than likely that the first time you had GORP it was made up of Good Old Raisins and Peanuts, and it probably tasted wonderful. But as we have refined our tastes somewhat, our GORP is now made up of equal measures of chocolate chips, cashews (or mixed nuts), and dried fruit pieces. It's not exactly lo-cal but it's almost instant energy.

D.J. Inman at the terminus of South Saint Vrain Trail near Baptist Camp.

PHOTO BY DAVE MULLER

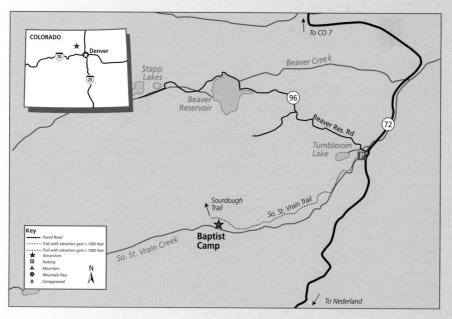

16. South Sourdough Trail

TOUR DISTANCE	5.5 miles one way
TOUR TIME	145 minutes
STARTING ELEVATION	10,070 feet
HIGHEST ELEVATION	10,200 feet
ELEVATION GAIN	850 feet (includes 720 extra feet)
DIFFICULTY	More difficult
AVALANCHE DANGER	Least
RELEVANT MAPS	Trails Illustrated Number 102
	Ward 7.5 minute
	Boulder County
	Roosevelt National Forest

GETTING THERE: Lower Trailhead: From Nederland, drive north on Colorado 72 for 7 miles and turn left onto the Rainbow Lakes Road (Number 298). Follow this road 0.5 mile to the trailhead on the right and park one vehicle in the large lot on the left. Upper Trailhead: In your second vehicle, drive back to Colorado 72. Turn left and drive 4.7 miles to Brainard Lake Road on the left. Drive up this road 2.5 miles to the Red Rock Trailhead and a wooden trailhead sign on the left. Park on the right 50 yards before the fee station.

COMMENT: The Sourdough Trail has northern, middle, and southern segments and runs north and south on the eastern side of the Brainard Lake area. This tour involves the southern part and a route from the upper to lower trailheads. Using two vehicles is recommended. The Brainard Lake area is often very windy, and exposed areas may lack snow in the winter. Therefore, this trail is best in its upper tree-covered parts and after a good fresh snowfall. If you are using only one trailhead, a good option is the upper segment down to and back from the Peace Bridge over Fourmile Creek, a distance of 3.1 miles each way.

THE TOUR: From the Red Rock trailhead sign, begin to the north northwest into the trees. The trail then rises and falls along the eastern flanks of Niwot Mountain before curving east to the lower trailhead on the Rainbow Lakes Road (Road 116). Blue diamond tree blazes mark the trail, which is closed to snowmobiles. There are occasional vistas to the south and east. At mile 3.1 you cross over Fourmile Creek on the narrow Peace Bridge. Continue southward another 0.75 mile to a trail sign and a 0.25 mile descent to an open area where the trail passes under power lines. In the lower 40 percent of this one-way descent, you may cross some areas with little snow due to the frequent winds.

North trailhead of South Sourdough Trail.

PHOTO BY DAVE MULLER

PHOTO BY DAVID HITE

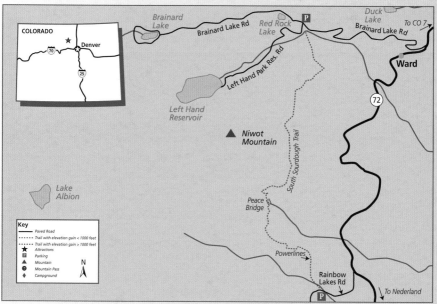

45

17. Big South Trail

TOUR DISTANCE	2.5 miles each way
TOUR TIME	Up in 77 minutes, down in 67 minutes (snowshoer's times)
STARTING ELEVATION	8,440 feet
HIGHEST ELEVATION	8,900 feet
ELEVATION GAIN	1,110 feet (includes 325 extra feet each way)
DIFFICULTY	More difficult
AVALANCHE DANGER	Least
RELEVANT MAPS	Trails Illustrated Number 112 Boston Peak 7.5 minute Chambers Lake 7.5 minute Larimer County Number Three Roosevelt National Forest

GETTING THERE: From U.S. 287 northwest of Fort Collins, drive west on Colorado 14 up Poudre Canyon for 46.9 miles. Park on the left at the Big South Trailhead.

COMMENT: The Big South Trail continues over 10 miles along the banks of the Cache Le Poudre River and ends in Rocky Mountain National Park at Poudre Lake near Milner Pass. This described trek extends only 2.5 miles to the bridge over May Creek. The flowing waters of the Poudre are the feature of this outing. Snowshoers should have little trouble on this trail, but it is not recommended for cross-country skiers due to its steep curving sections along the narrow trail.

THE TOUR: Start off to the south and reach the Comanche Peak Wilderness boundary after 0.5 mile. Continue as the trail rises and falls with the Poudre River always on the right. Pass six side trails to camp sites before reaching the bridge crossing over May Creek. This is the turnaround point for this described trek as the trail continues. Be careful on your return especially with the occasional steep drop-offs beside the trail.

SIDEBAR: DOG RULES AND PROTOCOLS

Part of the fun of a winter outing is taking the dog along. But we'd ask you to consider several thoughts before you take Rex onto a quiet winter trail. Please think about control and safety. Can you keep Rex under control? It's a safe bet no one appreciates your dog as much as you do. It's an even safer bet that you don't want Rex jumping up on them or interfering with their backcountry experience. Need we add that it's just not good if Rex chases wildlife. So if you can't control him with a whistle or a shout, leave him at home. If you do bring Rex, make sure he's in good enough shape to handle a snowy winter trail. We knew one Sheepdog-Wolfhound mix who would stand on our skis when we took a break to tell us it was time to turn around.

D.J. Inman and Frank Beghtel at Big South Trailhead.

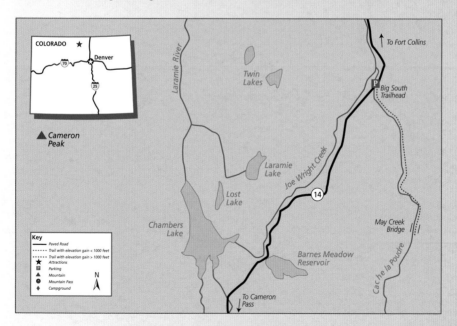

47

18. Cameron Connection

TOUR DISTANCE	2.3 miles each way
TOUR TIME	Up in 90 minutes, down in 62 minutes.
STARTING ELEVATION	9,990 feet
HIGHEST ELEVATION	10,320 feet
ELEVATION GAIN	1,090 feet (includes 380 extra feet each way)
DIFFICULTY	Easiest
AVALANCHE DANGER	Least
RELEVANT MAPS	Cameron Pass Cross-Country Trail Map Trails Illustrated Number 112 Clark Peak 7.5 minute Larimer County Number Three Roosevelt National Forest

GETTING THERE: From U.S. 287 northwest of Fort Colllns, drive west on Colorado 14 for 56.1 miles. Park on the left at the Zimmerman Lake parking area.

COMMENT: The Cameron Connection is a well-marked winter trail which culminates on Cameron Pass. The pass is named after General Robert A. Cameron, whose many exploits included the founding of Fort Collins. The Cameron Pass area usually has good winter snow depth. The trail is one of several in the Cameron Pass area. It winds through the trees parallel to Colorado Highway 14 for over 2 miles between the pass and the Zimmerman Lake parking area below.

THE TOUR: To begin, cross over Colorado 14 to a trailhead sign 30 yards below the parking lot. Enter the trees to the north northwest and take the left fork at a sign within 50 feet of the trailhead sign. Follow the blue diamond tree blazes to the south. Proceed upward and follow a curve to the right and then to the left through the forest. The trail rises and falls, passing through a few meadows with blue pole markers before reaching an upper trailhead sign at Cameron Pass near a parking area and rest rooms. On clear days, the Nokhu Crags are impressive on the left and the Diamond Peaks above on the right. The return back to the lower trailhead provides some gliding opportunities for the skier, but the trail makes frequent turns and provides few straightaways.

SIDEBAR: EXTRA FOOD

On a day trip, skiers and snowshoers often carry a lunch. We are fond of peanut better and jelly on a bagel or pita bread because they don't get all smashed up in the pack. Regardless of what you take for lunch, toss in some nutrition bars. Add a candy bar or two and an apple or orange, all of which pack and travel well in plastic bags. You never know when you will be out longer than you think.

The Nokhu Crags from Cameron Connection.

PHOTO BY DAVE MULLER

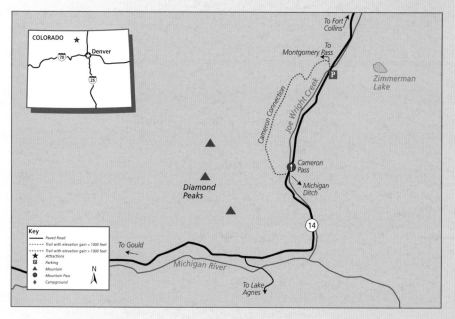

49

19. Joe Wright Trail

TOUR DISTANCE	1.7 miles (total for both loops)
TOUR TIME	43 minutes (total for both loops in snowshoer's time)
STARTING ELEVATION	9,880 feet
HIGHEST ELEVATION	10,000 feet
LOWEST ELEVATION	9,650 feet
ELEVATION GAIN	655 feet (includes 305 extra feet)
DIFFICULTY	Easiest
AVALANCHE DANGER	Least
RELEVANT MAPS	Trails Illustrated Number 112 Chambers Lake 7.5 minute Clark Peak 7.5 minute Larimer County Number Three Roosevelt National Forest

GETTING THERE: From U.S. 287 northwest of Fort Collins, drive west on Colorado 14 up Poudre Canyon for 53.5 miles. Park on the left in the Joe Wright Reservoir parking area.

COMMENT: This is the easiest winter tour in the beautiful Cameron Pass area. The Joe Wright Trail consists of two loops in a figure-eight pattern. These can be traversed in less than an hour. There is usually good snow in this area until late March.

THE TOUR: From the trailhead signboard on the north side of Colorado 14, 200 yards east of the parking area, begin to the north northwest and keep left as the loop begins. Follow the blue diamond markers over gentle terrain past the high point of this trek and soon reach a fork with arrows pointing left and right. Left is the upper loop. Descend to the right (southeast) to another fork at the lowest point of the loop. Go left (east) here and complete the upper loop at the fork you encountered earlier. Go left here (southeast) and descend again to the fork at the low point. Then go to the right (south) and gradually ascend through the forest to complete the loop, and then go left back to the starting point. Comanche Peak lies to the southwest beyond Colorado 14 and the Joe Wright Reservoir.

SIDEBAR: GAITERS

As you know, gaiters are coverings for the boot and lower leg. If truth be known, they are unnecessary unless you are breaking trail. Gaiters come in three basic sizes: short ones that cover your boot tops and ankles, full-length ones that cover most of your boot and lower leg, and super gaiters, which are strictly winter mountaineering gear. The best bet for breaking trail are full-sized gaiters.

Joe Wright Trailhead near Cameron Pass.

PHOTO BY DAVE MULLER

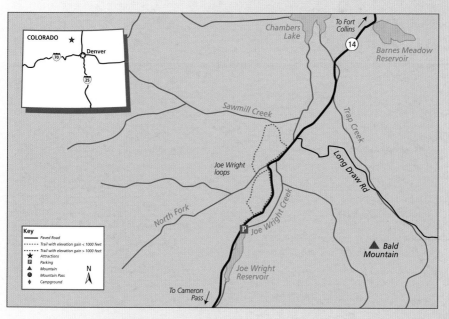

51

20. Lake Agnes

TOUR DISTANCE	2.8 miles each way
TOUR TIME	Up in 80 minutes, down in 58 minutes
STARTING ELEVATION	9,720 feet
HIGHEST ELEVATION	10,677 feet
ELEVATION GAIN	1,177 feet (includes 220 extra feet)
DIFFICULTY	Most difficult
AVALANCHE DANGER	Moderate over the last 0.5 mile
RELEVANT MAPS	Trails Illustrated Numbers 112 and 200 Cameron Pass Cross-Country Trail Map Clark Peak 7.5 minute Mount Richthofen 7.5 minute Larimer County Number Three

GETTING THERE: Trailhead parking lies along the south side of Colorado 14, 2.5 miles west of Cameron Pass (which is 57.5 miles west of U.S. 287 via Colorado 14).

COMMENT: Located in the Colorado State Forest, the trek to Lake Agnes is steep but rewarding. The cross-country skier and snowshoer are likely to arrive at the lake at approximately the same time. The return trip, of course, can be much faster for the skier. The rewards include the great views of the very striking Nokhu Crags and Mount Richthofen above the lake and the Agnes Cabin 2 miles from the trailhead. This small cabin can be rented throughout the year.

THE TOUR: Begin from the parking area down the road to the east. After 75 yards, pass under or around a road barrier. After another 75 yards, you reach a low point. Avoid the side road on the right. Continue on the main road past a summer fee collection station until you reach a sign and road fork 0.7 mile from the trailhead. Go right and cross the headwaters of the Michigan River on a bridge before ascending the wide road. At mile 0.8 from Colorado 14, pass the road to the Crags Campground on the left and continue up the steep road through patchy forest. It is another 1.1 miles of ascent before you emerge into a clearing known as the Crags Scenic Area. The Agnes Cabin and an outbuilding are here to the right of the trail. Many will turn around here because the final stretch to the lake is very steep. This last 0.75 mile segment follows the outflow creek from Lake Agnes and is very demanding. It requires climbing skins for the skier. Icy or crusty snow conditions will increase the challenge. The steep slopes of the Nokhu Crags loom above on the left. After reaching a snowy bench, gently descend 100 yards to frozen Lake Agnes, with its distinctive island in the middle. Mount Richthofen is impressive to the southeast. Be careful on your steep descent, especially to the Agnes Cabin area.

A frozen Lake Agnes with Mount Richthofen in the background. PHOTO BY DAVE MULLER

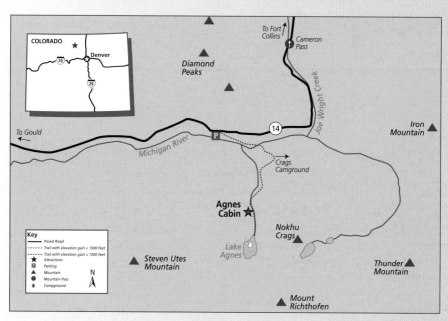

21. Meadows Trail to Zimmerman Lake

TOUR DISTANCE	4.5 miles each way
TOUR TIME	Up in 140 minutes, down in 92 minutes
STARTING ELEVATION	9,360 feet
HIGHEST ELEVATION	10,500 feet
ELEVATION GAIN	1,970 feet (includes 415 extra feet each way)
DIFFICULTY	Most difficult
AVALANCHE DANGER	Least
RELEVANT MAPS	Trails Illustrated Number 112 Chambers Lake 7.5 minute Larimer County Number Three Roosevelt National Forest

GETTING THERE: From the junction with U.S. 287, northwest of Fort Collins, drive west on Colorado 14 up beautiful Poudre Canyon for 52.6 miles. Park in the lot on the left near a Long Draw trailhead sign. (This lot is 0.9 mile north of Long Draw Road.)

COMMENT: Two cross-country ski and snowshoe trails lead to Zimmerman Lake in the Neota Wilderness, north of Cameron Pass. One is short (1.5 miles) and steep and rises from Colorado 14 to the east. The other is the Meadows Trail and will be described here. It is longer, more demanding, and proceeds in a southerly direction from Colorado 14, north of the Long Draw Road. This trail is marked by blue tree blazes, poles, occasional arrows on tree trunks and a few signs. Snowmobiles are forbidden in the wilderness area, and dogs should be kept on a leash.

THE TOUR: From the parking area, descend slightly southeast to the trail and continue 0.5 mile up to the right through the trees to the Long Draw Road. Turn left on the Long Draw Road, go 40 yards, and then exit onto a road ascending to the right (southeast). After about 250 yards, take the trail on the right at a signed fork and ascend to the southwest. You will quickly reach an unmarked intersection of two trails. Take either one as they reconnect just before the trail curves sharply to the right and steepens. At this curve, the skier can put on climbing skins to make the ascent easier. Rise through the woods and then pass through several small meadows as the trail relentlessly rises to finally reach a junction with the other Zimmerman Lake Trail, just west of the lake. Go left 75 yards to reach the large frozen lake with some unnamed peaks of the Never Summer Range to the east. Return to the original trailhead by your ascent trail, with its many up and down segments.

Long shadows on Zimmerman Lake.

PHOTO BY DAVE MULLER

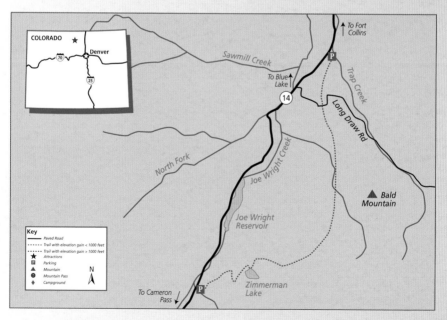

22. Michigan Ditch

TOUR DISTANCE	2.2 miles each way
TOUR TIME	Out in 50 minutes, back in 49 minutes
STARTING ELEVATION	10,255 feet (Cameron Pass)
HIGHEST ELEVATION	10,320 feet
ELEVATION GAIN	85 feet (includes an extra 10 feet each way)
DIFFICULTY	Easiest
RELEVANT MAPS	Cameron Pass Cross-Country Trail Map
	Trails Illustrated Number 112
	Clark Peak 7.5 minute
	Chambers Lake 7.5 minute
	Larimer County Number Three

GETTING THERE: From U.S. 287 northwest of Fort Collins, drive west on Colorado 14 up Poudre Canyon for 57.8 miles to Cameron Pass. Park in the designated area on the right (west) side of the road.

COMMENT: The lovely drive from Fort Collins up Poudre Canyon to Cameron Pass provides some beautiful scenery. At the pass, however, your special treat is the magnificent Nokhu Crags, which loom above to the southwest. An easy trek parallels an aqueduct known as the Michigan Ditch. A Colorado State Park usage fee is required. Maps are available on signboards along the initial part of the route.

THE TOUR: Be careful crossing Colorado 14. Begin from the east side of the highway to the southeast on a wide road into the forest. Avoid the occasional side roads and stay fairly level along the aqueduct. After 1 mile, you pass several primitive cabins. Continue generally south in scenic open terrain until you reach a four-way intersection 2.2 miles from the trailhead. A sign for American Lakes and Thunder Pass will be on your left. This can be your turnaround point unless you want to explore the other three options. The lovely mountains to the northwest are known as the Diamond Peaks.

SIDEBAR: WATCHING THE WEATHER

Fire up your computer before you leave the house and check the most recent radar images of the state, and particularly your specific destination. Check the 24-hour weather forecast on the Web or TV and then go prepared for anything. Once there, stay aware of changing weather conditions. From your morning research, you'll know if any serious weather systems are headed your way. Watch the sky for horsetails high aloft that indicate more difficult weather is on the way, and consider wearing a watch that includes a barometer. Rising barometric pressure is good. Falling barometric pressure means you might want to head for home—either that or dig a snow cave.

TOP: The dramatic Nokhu Crags can be seen from the Michigan Ditch. PHOTO BY TERRY ROOT
BOTTOM: Frank Beghtel on the Michigan Ditch Trail at the fork to American Lakes. PHOTO BY DAVE MULLER

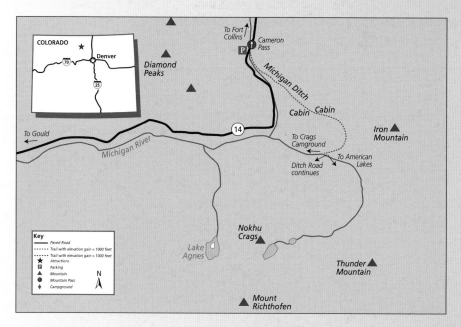

23. Montgomery Pass

TOUR DISTANCE	1.9 miles each way
TOUR TIME	Up in 76 minutes, down in 45 minutes
STARTING ELEVATION	9,990 feet
HIGHEST ELEVATION	10,990 feet
ELEVATION GAIN	1,280 feet (includes 140 extra feet each way)
DIFFICULTY	Most difficult
AVALANCHE DANGER	Moderate (upper half)
RELEVANT MAPS	Trails Illustrated Number 112 Clark Peak 7.5 minute Cameron Pass Cross-Country Trail Map Larimer County Number Three

GETTING THERE: From northwest of Fort Collins, where U.S. 287 heads northwest toward Wyoming and Colorado 14 begins its long westerly ascent of lovely Poudre Canyon, drive 56.2 miles on Colorado 14 and park on the left in the Zimmerman Lake parking area. Cameron Pass is 1.4 miles further on Colorado 14.

COMMENT: The trek to Montgomery Pass is one of the most difficult in the splendid group of winter trails in the Cameron Pass area west of Fort Collins. A steep ascent to the pass rewards the nordic skier and snowshoer with a breathtaking panorama and extensive open terrain and snow-filled bowls to explore. Stay on the direct route to the pass to avoid any avalanche danger around timberline. The nordic skier may wish to use climbing skins for the ascent. Snowmobiles are very unlikely on this steep, narrow and winding trail.

THE TOUR: Carry your skis or snowshoes across the highway from the parking area. Put on your gear and enter the trees to the north northwest past a signboard and register. Quickly pass a trail on the left called the Cameron Connection. Continue straight before the trail turns sharply to the left (southwest) and continues its inexorable climb toward timberline through thick forest. After 1.3 miles, heading west, you reach a small clearing. You're faced with two options: a trail ascending to the left and one that enters the trees on the right. The left route ascends steeply to a beautiful overlook of the Nokhu Crags and the Never Summer Range. The right fork is the direct route and continues through the trees as the trail curves back and forth with the Montgomery Creek drainage always on your right (north). The route is not well marked. Hopefully, you will have some tracks to follow. Soon the trees become less abundant, and the pass comes into view to the west. Climb the open, often windblown, slopes to a wooden sign and great views at the pass. The return can be rapid. Enjoy the ski gliding but watch out for trekkers coming up the trail lest you collide.

The open terrain of Montgomery Pass.

PHOTO BY DAVE MULLER

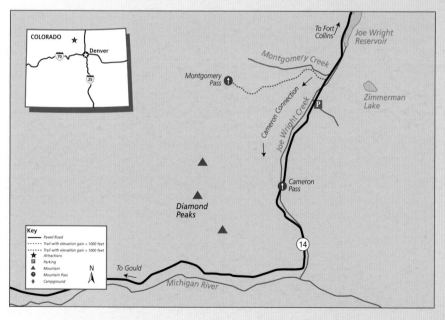

24. Zimmerman Lake Loop

TOUR DISTANCE	3.4 miles (total loop)
TOUR TIME	Up to high point in 46 minutes, down in 48 minutes
STARTING ELEVATION	10,010 feet
HIGHEST ELEVATION	10,560 feet
ELEVATION GAIN	750 feet (includes 200 extra feet)
DIFFICULTY	More difficult
AVALANCHE DANGER	Least
RELEVANT MAPS	Trails Illustrated Number 112 Clark Peak 7.5 minutes Chambers Lake 7.5 minute Larimer County Number Three Roosevelt National Forest

GETTING THERE: Drive on Colorado 14 either 56.2 miles west from U.S. 287 northwest of Fort Collins or 1.4 miles east from Cameron Pass. Park in the large lot on the southern side of the highway at the trailhead.

COMMENT: Zimmerman Lake, near Cameron Pass in north central Colorado, is the primary spawning area for the state fish, the Greenback Cutthroat Trout. Eggs from this lake are taken to stock other lakes throughout the state. The tour uses a four-wheel drive road up to the lake. A forest trail circles the large lake amid great scenery and connects with the ascent road.

THE TOUR: Begin south from the signboard and trail register. Maps may also be available here. After 50 yards through open terrain, enter the trees at the large sign about Colorado's state fish. Follow the road as it rises and curves to the left. The way is steep at times as the blue diamond markers on trees guide you up the snake-like road to a sign and fork at a clearing 1.1 miles from the trailhead. This is where your clockwise loop trip will rejoin this road. Continue up the left fork into the forest for another 0.2 mile to another signed fork. The trail on the right leads quickly to Zimmerman Lake. Take the left fork on the narrower trail, which circles the lake in a clockwise direction. Be sure to follow the blue diamonds. It is very easy to become lost in this vast basin. With an unnamed peak to the east, the loop trail affords intermittent overviews of the lake before descending an open gully to rejoin the main road which you ascended. Go left on this road and, if you are on skis, enjoy the good downhill gliding back to the trailhead.

One of the many great panoramas across Zimmerman Lake.

PHOTO BY DAVE MULLER

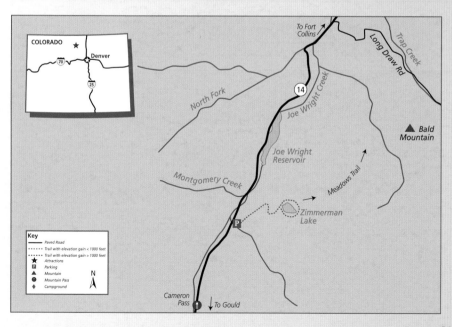

61

25. Chief Mountain

TOUR DISTANCE	1.5 miles each way
TOUR TIME	Up in 68 minutes, down in 38 minutes (snowshoer's time)
STARTING ELEVATION	10,680 feet
HIGHEST ELEVATION	11,709 feet
ELEVATION GAIN	1,129 feet (includes an extra 50 feet each way)
DIFFICULTY	More difficult
AVALANCHE DANGER	Least
RELEVANT MAPS	Trails Illustrated Number 104 Idaho Springs 7.5 minute Clear Creek County Arapaho National Forest

GETTING THERE: From Colorado 74 between Bergen Park and Evergreen, drive west on Squaw Pass Road, which becomes Colorado 103, for 12.2 miles. Park on the right.

COMMENT: Chief Mountain is a good destination throughout the year. Its proximity to Denver and Evergreen make this trek a delightful half-day outing. Snowshoes are recommended, but an experienced cross-country skier can enjoy this trail as well. The views from the rocky, windblown summit reward your effort. Look north northwest to Longs Peak, east northeast to Squaw Mountain, southeast to Pikes Peak, and southwest to Mount Evans.

THE TOUR: Cross the road and begin your ascent to the southeast at a marker. If the snow isn't too deep, a stone marker with the number 290 will be visible and is quickly passed as the trail zigzags through the trees to a four-way intersection after 0.4 mile. Continue the ascent by proceeding straight (southeast) past a Chief Mountain sign on the right. After another 0.3 mile through the forest, you reach a saddle between Papoose Mountain on the left and Chief Mountain to the right. Continue up to the south for about 100 yards. The trail then curves sharply to the right (northwest). Traverse the pine forest until you reach a treeless area below the summit. Switchbacks then lead to the base of the high point. Take off your skis or snowshoes here and carefully ascend the rocks. Enjoy great summit vistas before the rapid return.

SIDEBAR: HEAD COVER

Even if you prefer to have your head uncovered, consider wearing a cap or hat on these winter trails. The sun can burn you and lots of body heat can be lost through your head and contribute to hypothermia.

Looking east from Chief Mountain Trail.

PHOTO BY DAVID HITE

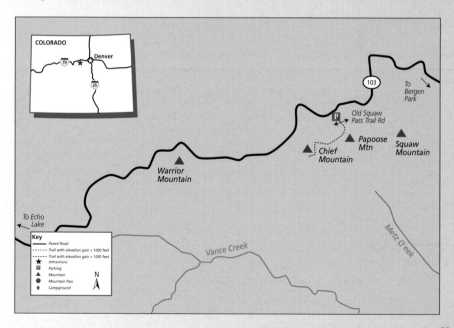

COLORADO

Denver

70

25

103

To
Bergen
Park

P Old Squaw
Pass Trail Rd

Papoose
Mtn

Squaw
Mountain

Chief
Mountain

Warrior
Mountain

To Echo
Lake

Metz Creek

Vance Creek

Key

Paved Road

Trail with elevation gain < 1000 feet

Trail with elevation gain > 1000 feet

★ Attractions

P Parking

▲ Mountain

Mountain Pass

Campground

N

63

26. Echo Lake

TOUR DISTANCE	1 mile (total loop)
TOUR TIME	30 minutes (snowshoer's time)
STARTING ELEVATION	10,597 feet
HIGHEST ELEVATION	10,597 feet
ELEVATION GAIN	Negligible
DIFFICULTY	Easiest
AVALANCHE DANGER	Least
RELEVANT MAPS	Trails Illustrated Number 104
	Mount Evans 7.5 minute
	Clear Creek County
	Arapaho National Forest

GETTING THERE: From Interstate 70 at Idaho Springs, drive south on Colorado 103 (the Chicago Basin Road) for 12.5 miles. Park on the right 30 yards past the Echo Lake Park sign on the right.

COMMENT: Clear Creek County is close to Metropolitan Denver and has several winter trails. One of these is the loop around Echo Lake. Echo Lake Park is one of the Denver Mountain Parks. Keep to the edge of the lake to avoid possible thin ice. This loop around large Echo Lake, beneath Mount Evans, has virtually no elevation gain.

THE TOUR: Begin on foot to the west with the lake on the left and a stone picnic shelter on the right. Follow the path as it curves to the left. Continue along the right side of the lake. Go to the left at a sign as the Chicago Lakes Trail continues straight ahead. Follow the edge of the lake in a counterclockwise direction past a picnic table and back to your starting point after a full mile.

SIDEBAR: HYPOTHERMIA

Hypothermia is a loss of core body temperature that affects muscle and mental functions. To prevent hypothermia, understand and protect yourself against wind chill factors, stay dry, and replenish fluids and food throughout the day. Remember that you lose a great deal of water through perspiration and respiration. Mild symptoms of hypothermia are uncontrollable shivering, impaired motor control, and very cold hands and feet because the body is trying to protect its core temperature. This person can still walk and talk, but is obviously in trouble. Get them more layers of dry clothing, keep them active, and head them toward shelter. More serious hypothermia symptoms are violent shivering, loss of motor control, incoherent or slurred speech, muddled consciousness, and a bad attitude.

The Mount Evans massif looms beyond snowshoers circling Echo Lake.

PHOTO BY TERRY ROOT

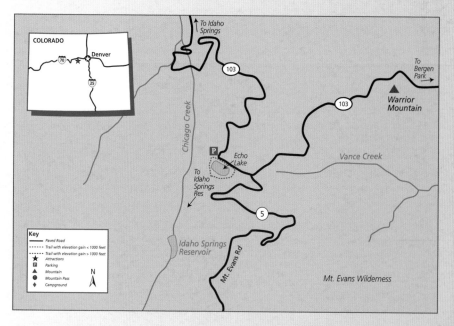

65

27. Idaho Springs Reservoir

TOUR DISTANCE	2.8 miles each way
TOUR TIME	Up in 83 minutes, down in 52 minutes
STARTING ELEVATION	9,470 feet
HIGHEST ELEVATION	10,617 feet
ELEVATION GAIN	1,147 feet
DIFFICULTY	More difficult
AVALANCHE DANGER	Least
RELEVANT MAPS	Trails Illustrated Number 104 Idaho Springs 7.5 minute Clear Creek County Arapaho National Forest

GETTING THERE: From Interstate 70 at exit 240 in Idaho Springs, drive south on Colorado 103 for 8.8 miles. Park off the road on the right just before the blocked side road on the right.

COMMENT: This trek to the Idaho Springs Reservoir lies close to Denver and makes a fine half-day outing. The little-used wide trail parallels Chicago Creek that joins Clear Creek down the valley at the town of Idaho Springs.

THE TOUR: Begin east northeast around the barrier up the side road. Do not be deterred by the sign at the barrier. The Arapaho National Forest staff affirm that this road is open to cross-country skiers and snowshoers. Ascend the winding road for 1.4 miles to a fork. The left path enters Shwayder Camp. Continue up the right fork. You will reach a clearing with some cabin ruins and the Chicago Lakes trail on the left after another mile. Continue straight, and you will soon pass some signs before reaching an overlook of the Idaho Springs Reservoir. Take a break before the easier return to Colorado 103.

SIDEBAR: BUYING GEAR

One of the many great things about cross-country skiing and snowshoeing is that nobody cares all that much about what you are wearing or what your gear looks like. Style points are often awarded for face plants or post-holing, but not for clothing or gear. We have always thought that dependable, well-made gear bought at the end of the season or bought used was the best way to go. At the end of the season, and for ski gear at the end of summer, you may have fewer choices in an outdoor store. But talk to the clerks; they are usually knowledgeable and will point out what's right for you given the kind of gear you want, what you are going to do with it, and what your skill level is.

Shwayder Camp enroute to Idaho Springs Reservoir.

PHOTO BY DAVE MULLER

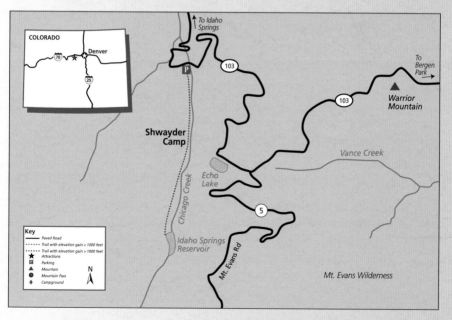

28. Mount Evans Road to Dos Chappell Nature Center

TOUR DISTANCE	2.9 miles each way
TOUR TIME	Up in 99 minutes, down in 57 minutes
STARTING ELEVATION	10,650 feet
HIGHEST ELEVATION	11,506 feet
ELEVATION GAIN	856 feet
DIFFICULTY	More difficult
AVALANCHE DANGER	Least
RELEVANT MAPS	Trails Illustrated Number 104 Idaho Springs 7.5 minute Clear Creek County Arapaho National Forest

GETTING THERE: From Interstate 70 at Idaho Springs, drive south on Colorado 103 for 12.8 miles. Park on the right near the barrier that blocks Colorado 5, the Mount Evans Road.

COMMENT: The Mount Evans Road is one of two Colorado roads that rise to the summits of Colorado Fourteeners. The gradual grade up the wide road provides a good winter outing for the snowshoer or cross-country skier when there is little wind and the snow is good. With the trailhead within 50 miles of central Denver and snowmobiles forbidden in the Mount Evans Wilderness, this road is an inviting destination.

THE TOUR: Begin up the Mount Evans Road after passing around the metal road barrier. Follow the road as it curves back and forth past markers for miles 1 and 2. At around 2.3 miles, the route emerges into a scenic open area with Mount Evans visible ahead. Just before the 3 mile marker as the road curves sharply to the right, you reach Mount Goliath Nature Center, a well-built wooden building, named in honor of Dos Chappell. This is the turnaround point, so enjoy the scenery and refresh before the gentle downhill return.

SIDEBAR: TRAIL PROTOCOL

There are a number of unwritten rules on the trails. We have always thought that the person or group coming downhill should have the right of way because you have less control going downhill than going uphill, particularly if you're a skier. Fast-moving groups should not bunch up behind slow-moving groups and make rude noises; instead, they should ask the slower movers if they can pass. Most people are happy to step aside for faster groups.

Skiers huddle on the lee side of the Nature Center building.

PHOTO BY DAVE MULLER

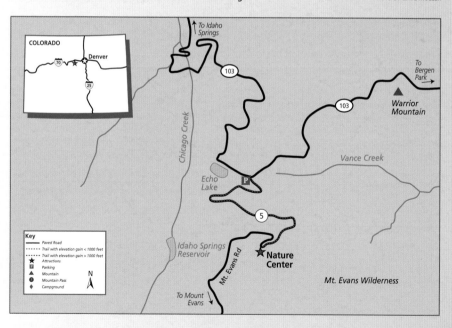

69

29. Pavilion Point

TOUR DISTANCE	3.6 miles each way
TOUR TIME	Up in 102 minutes, down in 60 minutes
STARTING ELEVATION	9,170 feet
HIGHEST ELEVATION	10,000 feet
ELEVATION GAIN	950 feet (includes 60 extra feet each way)
DIFFICULTY	Easiest
AVALANCHE DANGER	Least
RELEVANT MAPS	Trails Illustrated Number 104
	Georgetown 7.5 minute
	Clear Creek County
	Arapaho National Forest

GETTING THERE: From Interstate 70 west of Georgetown at Silver Plume, take exit 226. On the unpaved frontage road on the south side of the road, drive west parallel to the highway for 0.4 mile and park on the right at a fork.

COMMENT: The tour to Pavilion Point, south of Georgetown and Silver Plume, uses the old railroad bed of the Argentine Central Railroad that once continued up Leavenworth Gulch to Waldorf and beyond. Snow depth can be a problem here until late January. Because the route is an overgrown railroad bed, the grade is easy and the path usually wide enough for a small train. Some route finding is necessary as you ascend the side slopes of Leavenworth Mountain.

THE TOUR: Begin up the road to the southeast through mixed evergreen and aspen forest. After 0.4 mile, pass a large water storage cylinder below on your left. Continue up the main road and keep straight at the four-way intersection with private property above on your right. Generally avoid the small side trails. You will pass an old mine chute on the right at mile 1.4 from the trailhead. Continue another 0.4 mile and take the sharp right fork. (A second mine chute is visible straight ahead, but that road is a dead end.) Continue up the road, and within 50 yards you will pass a side road rising to the left. Continue on the right fork and descend a bit before resuming your gradual uphill direction. Very quickly you will cross a drainage with a brief steep downhill segment and a mine remnant below on your right. After negotiating this difficult segment, you soon reach a sharp bend in the trail to the left. It will be another 1.5 miles from here to the solitary 30-foot chimney at Pavilion Point. Along this entire trek, there are occasional views down to Silver Plume and the 1-70 corridor. At Pavilion Point, the road continues another 1 mile to a connection with the road ascending Leavenworth Gulch. There is an overlook 25 yards up to the north northwest from the chimney.

The chimney at Pavilion Point.

PHOTO BY DAVE MULLER

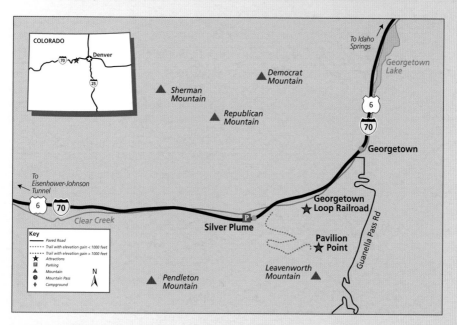

30. Saint Mary's Glacier Loop

TOUR DISTANCE	1.8 miles (total loop)
TOUR TIME	Up in 31 minutes, down in 36 minutes. (snowshoer's time)
STARTING ELEVATION	10,395 feet
HIGHEST ELEVATION	10,960 feet
ELEVATION GAIN	590 feet (includes 25 extra feet)
DIFFICULTY	Easiest
AVALANCHE DANGER	Moderate at and above Saint Mary's Lake
RELEVANT MAPS	Trails Illustrated Number 103 Empire 7.5 minute Clear Creek County Arapaho National Forest

GETTING THERE: From Interstate 70, west of Idaho Springs, take exit 238 and drive 0.2 mile on the north side of I-70 to the Fall River Road. Follow the Fall River Road for 8.9 miles to the trailhead on the left. Continue on the main road for another 0.1 mile and park in the plowed area on the left.

COMMENT: Saint Mary's Glacier is actually a permanent snowfield and not a glacier. Nonetheless, it makes a scenic destination for a winter, as well as a summer, tour. Located not far from Idaho Springs, the snowfield and Saint Mary's Lake can be reached by a short, steep trail with a loop return to the starting point.

THE TOUR: From the parking area, backtrack on the road for 0.1 mile. Then begin up to the north northeast from the trail sign. Ascend steeply up the road and soon enter the forest. Keep to the left of Fox Mountain, which will be visible ahead on the right side of Saint Mary's Lake. When you break out of the forest, continue to the north with the outlet of Saint Mary's Lake on your left and a metal bridge on the right. Persist upward to a rocky area with Saint Mary's Glacier and the valley above to the west northwest. Enjoy the views in all directions before returning to the metal bridge. From here you can retrace your ascent route. For the loop return, however, proceed to the left (southeast) and descend with the creek on the right. Pass an old mining artifact to a road that leads down to a four-way intersection. Go to the right (south southeast) and follow the road 0.5 mile back to the parking area.

SIDEBAR: GLACIERS VERSUS PERMANENT SNOWFIELDS

A glacier is essentially a long lasting river of ice that is formed on land and moves in response to gravity. A permanent snowfield is an extensive terrain covered by a smooth area of snow. We have permanent snowfields in Colorado.

Snowboarders trundle up Saint Mary's Glacier above the route in this book.

PHOTO BY TERRY ROOT

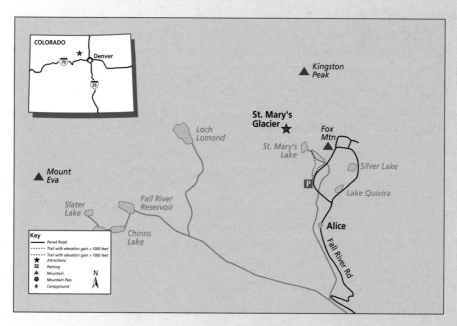

31. South Chicago Creek

TOUR DISTANCE	1.2 miles each way
TOUR TIME	Up in 36 minutes. Down in 18 minutes
STARTING ELEVATION	9,452 feet
HIGHEST ELEVATION	10,280 feet
ELEVATION GAIN	848 feet (includes 10 extra feet each way)
DIFFICULTY	More difficult
AVALANCHE DANGER	Least
RELEVANT MAPS	Trails Illustrated Number 104 Idaho Springs 7.5 minute Georgetown 7.5 minute Clear Creek County Arapaho National Forest

GETTING THERE: From Interstate 70 in Idaho Springs, drive south on Colorado 103 for 8.6 miles and park off the road on the right at a side road with a stop sign and a dead-end sign.

COMMENT: South Chicago Creek flows into Chicago Creek, which empties into Clear Creek at Idaho Springs. This tour parallels South Chicago Creek up to the Mount Evans Wilderness boundary. The wide road ascends relentlessly past two forks and provides a fast return, especially for the cross-country skier.

THE TOUR: Start up the side road to the southwest. Pass a series of cabins on the left and reach a fork after 0.7 mile. Continue to the right (southwest) another 0.4 mile to a second fork. Go left here another 200 yards to the road's end and a Mount Evans Wilderness boundary sign. This is the turnaround point for this route. A trail continues southwest into the wilderness and ascends steeply 1.5 miles before ending near timberline.

SIDEBAR: TREE WELLS

Blowing and drifting snow forms pits around the base of evergreens that are called tree wells. In an emergency when you need to get out of the weather, a tree well will afford you some protection from the wind and cold. But try to stay out of tree wells in normal conditions. If you have ever fallen into one by accident you know that extricating yourself from a tree well can be difficult, particularly if you don't have help.

A skier descending the gentle, sloped road along South Chicago Creek.

PHOTO BY TERRY ROOT

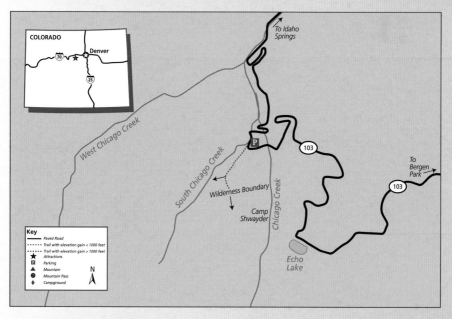

32. Squaw Mountain Fire Lookout

TOUR DISTANCE	1.5 miles each way
TOUR TIME	Up in 60 minutes, down in 38 minutes
STARTING ELEVATION	10,620 feet
HIGHEST ELEVATION	11,486 feet
ELEVATION GAIN	866 feet
DIFFICULTY	More difficult
AVALANCHE DANGER	Least
RELEVANT MAPS	Trails Illustrated Numbers 100 and 104 Idaho Springs 7.5 minute Squaw Pass 7.5 minute Clear Creek County Arapaho National Forest

GETTING THERE: From Interstate 70, take exit 252 and drive southwest on Colorado 74 for 3.3 miles. Turn right onto Squaw Pass Road (which becomes Colorado 103 after 8.5 miles) and set your mileage at zero. Continue west up this winding road for 12 miles from Colorado 74. Park off road at the side road on the left.

COMMENT: This half-day trek to the Squaw Mountain Fire Lookout Tower is not far from downtown Denver and offers a great panorama at the top. However, the wide road to the top is steep in spots, and the upper section of this outing is often wind-blown with little snow cover. If you need to remove your skis or snowshoes near the summit, the walk up to the fire lookout tower will provide scenic rewards. The best time to try this outing is after a recent local snowfall.

THE TOUR: Start up the wide road to the north northeast. After 0.4 mile, continue to ascend straight ahead at a four-way intersection. The Squaw Mountain Fire Lookout can now be seen, if visibility permits. Soon the road snakes up to the left and then to the right to reach a road barrier at 0.9 mile. Pass around or under the barrier and continue straight up the steep road. There are several switchbacks as you rise higher. Near the top, go right (southeast) at a road intersection and within 150 yards reach the end of the road at the foot of Squaw Mountain. Take off your skis or snowshoes and walk the rocky trail to a conical stone marker just below the fire lookout, which is closed to the public. Check out the views in every direction before the quicker return trip. Mount Evans lies to the southwest and Pikes Peak to the southeast. If the rocks along the way threaten your skis or snowshoes, take them off and walk the difficult segments on your return.

Linda Grey and Tua at the Squaw Mountain fire lookout.

PHOTO BY TERRY ROOT

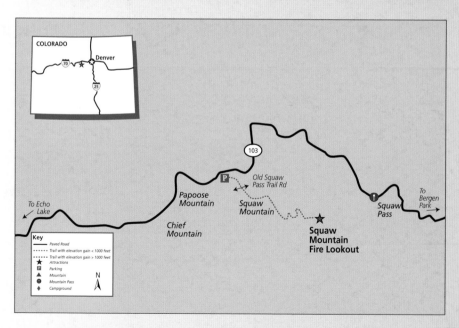

33. Bonfils Stanton Loop

TOUR DISTANCE	1.5 miles (total loop)
TOUR TIME	31 minutes
STARTING ELEVATION	9,230 feet
HIGHEST ELEVATION	9,400 feet
ELEVATION GAIN	185 feet (includes 15 extra feet)
DIFFICULTY	Easiest
AVALANCHE DANGER	Least
RELEVANT MAPS	Trails Illustrated Number 103
	Fraser 7.5 minute
	East Portal 7.5 minute
	Grand County Number Four
	Arapaho National Forest

GETTING THERE: On U.S. 40 at the southern edge of Winter Park, park off the east side of the highway near the Bonfils Stanton Outdoor Center sign. This area lies across the highway from the southern entrance to Winter Park Ski Area.

COMMENT: The Bonfils Stanton Outdoor Center offers two connecting trails that comprise a complete loop. The Challenger Trail joins the Discovery Trail and brings you back to the trailhead after an easy circuit around the edge of the willows near Jim Creek. A clockwise direction will be described. This is an ideal loop for families and beginning winter trekkers.

THE TOUR: The loop begins to the north northeast on the Challenger Trail, which curves to the right into the forest. After 0.3 mile, cross a bridge over a large water pipe. Continue with the willows on the right and soon connect with the Discovery Trail. Briefly cross the Jim Creek Trail and descend the Discovery Trail down to a four-way intersection. (You also can reach this point on the Jim Creek Trail after passing under the large water pipe.) From this junction, continue west over the boardwalk back to the loop starting point.

SIDEBAR: NATIONAL SPORTS CENTER FOR THE DISABLED

The National Sports Center for the Disabled (NSCD), which is housed at the Bonfils Stanton Outdoor Center, began in 1970 as a one-time ski lesson for children with amputations for the Children's Hospital of Denver. Today, the NSCD is one of the largest outdoor therapeutic recreation agencies in the world. Each year, thousands of children and adults with disabilities take to the ski slopes, mountain trails, and golf courses to learn more about sports—and themselves.

The large water pipe that you will see on this easy route.

PHOTO BY DAVE MULLER

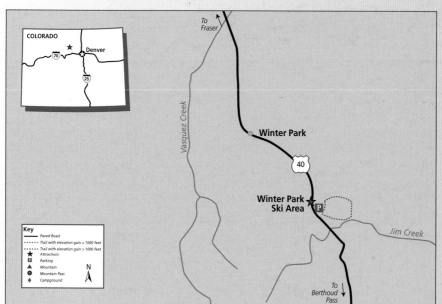

34. Byers Peak Trailhead

TOUR DISTANCE	4.8 miles each way
TOUR TIME	Up in 168 minutes, down in 78 minutes
STARTING ELEVATION	9,060 feet
HIGHEST ELEVATION	10,510 feet
ELEVATION GAIN	1,570 feet (includes 60 extra feet each way)
DIFFICULTY	More difficult
AVALANCHE DANGER	Moderate
RELEVANT MAPS	Trails Illustrated Number 103 Bottle Pass 7.5 minute Grand County Number Four Arapaho National Forest

GETTING THERE: From U.S. 40 at the traffic light in Fraser, take Grand County Road 72 to the southwest. After 0.3 mile, turn right onto Fraser Parkway. After 0.8 mile on this road, go left on Grand County Road 73. Follow this wide road west for 4.2 miles to a four-way intersection and some signs. Turn right here and park at the end of the road near the trailhead signs.

COMMENT: The vistas are few on this outing because you are mostly in thick, ever-green forest. Byers Peak comes into view at times in the final third of the trek. Byers Peak is the dominant and striking mountain to the west of Fraser.

THE TOUR: Start from the trailhead signs and proceed southwest for about 150 yards to a road, and then 300 yards south southwest to a signed fork. Take the left fork and continue south southwest, pass a slope with well-spaced evergreens on the left and descend gently to the crossing of West Saint Louis Creek. At any confusing intersec-tions, stay on the main road and ascend. At mile 2.6 from the trailhead, your route forks at a sign and an open road barrier. Take the right fork up to the west. After 0.3 mile from this fork, avoid a side road on the left and continue straight up the main road. Another mile brings you to a fork as the main road curves sharply to the right (north). Soon the road curves severely to the left (south) as a side trail leads off on the right. Before long, the road becomes shelf-like as you enter a high, heavily tim-bered bowl with some steep drop-offs on your left. This is the short area of moder-ate avalanche danger. Ascend to another sharp curve in the road; this one rises steeply to the right. It is another 0.75 mile from here to the end of the road at the Byers Peak Trail signboard and high point of this tour.

TOP: Byers Peak.   BOTTOM: The Byers Peak Trailhead route.

PHOTO BY DAVE MULLER

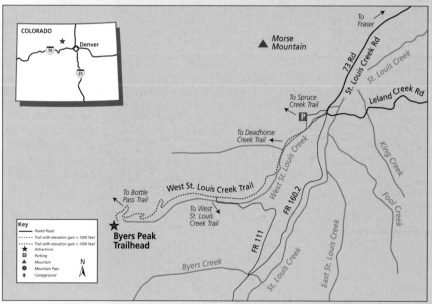

35. Deadhorse Creek

TOUR DISTANCE	4.2 miles each way
TOUR TIME	Up in 125 minutes, down in 64 minutes
STARTING ELEVATION	9,060 feet
HIGHEST ELEVATION	10,055 feet
ELEVATION GAIN	1,095 feet (includes 50 extra feet each way)
DIFFICULTY	Easiest
AVALANCHE DANGER	Least
RELEVANT MAPS	Trails Illustrated Number 103 Bottle Pass 7.5 minute Grand County Number Four Arapaho National Forest

GETTING THERE: From the traffic light in Fraser, drive north 0.2 mile on U.S. 40 and turn left onto Eisenhower Drive. Cross the railroad tracks and follow Eisenhower Drive as it becomes Carriage Drive and curves left to reach Grand County Road 73 (0.4 mile from U.S. 40). Turn right and continue up the valley on Road 73 for 4.3 miles to a four-way intersection. Turn right, continue 0.1 mile, and park at the trailhead signs.

COMMENT: The wide, gradually ascending Deadhorse Creek Road, west of Fraser, in the Fraser Experimental Forest, is ideal for the cross-country skier and snowshoer. However, the good downhill runs on the return are the skier's bonus. Other positive features are the absence of forbidden snowmobiles and glorious vistas in the higher areas. Several other trails are also nearby. Please do not interfere with any equipment in the Fraser Experimental Forest.

THE TOUR: From the trailhead signs, begin to the west southwest. Avoid any side trails and reach a road after 150 yards. Go to the right (southwest) on this road and reach a signed intersection within 0.5 mile of the trailhead. Descend the right fork and cross West Saint Louis Creek. Ascend parallel to Deadhorse Creek in a series of switchbacks. Stay on the ascending, main road and keep right at all intersections. The terminus of this outing is reached as a marked, narrow trail leaves the road and descends northeast into the forest on the right. (For a more demanding and faster return to your trailhead, take this Spruce Creek Trail.) Enjoy the panorama with Bottle Peak to the southwest before retracing your ascent route on the steadily downhill road.

Frank Beghtel cruises up the Dead Horse Creek Road.

PHOTO BY DAVE MULLER

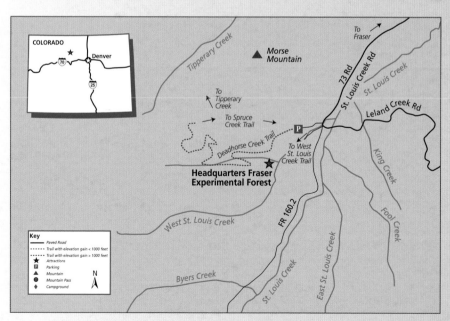

36. Deadhorse Creek – Spruce Creek Loop

TOUR DISTANCE	Up in 1.8 miles, down in 4.2 miles
TOUR TIME	Up in 105 minutes, down in 80 minutes
STARTING ELEVATION	9,032 feet
HIGHEST ELEVATION	10,260 feet
ELEVATION GAIN	1,303 feet (includes 75 total extra feet)
DIFFICULTY	More difficult
AVALANCHE DANGER	Least
RELEVANT MAPS	Trails Illustrated Number 103 Bottle Pass 7.5 minute Grand County Number Four Arapaho National Forest

GETTING THERE: From the traffic light in Fraser, drive north on U.S. 40 for 0.2 mile, turn left onto Eisenhower Drive, and set your mileage to zero. Drive west across the railroad tracks as Eisenhower Drive becomes Carriage Drive and curves left to join County Road 73 at a "T" (0.4 mile from U.S. 40). Turn right and follow County Road 73 (the Saint Louis Creek Road) straight up the valley to a parking area on the right at mile 4.7 from U.S. 40.

COMMENT: The Deadhorse Creek Loop is one of several good cross-country skiing and snowshoe routes southwest of Fraser. Unless you prefer steep downhill descents on a narrower trail, try this loop in a counterclockwise direction. This enables you to ascend the steep, shorter, and narrower Spruce Creek Trail and enjoy a long, gradual skier's glide down the wide Deadhorse Creek Road.

THE TOUR: This loop begins to the southwest on the Spruce Creek Trail just before the parking area. The trail ascends through the trees and is steep at times. After 1.1 miles with Spruce Creek always on the left, you reach a signed fork and a road barrier on the left. You continue straight (east southeast), around the barrier, and ascend a steeper 0.7 mile to reach the Deadhorse Creek Road. This is the highest point of the loop. Now descend to the left (south southwest) and follow the wide road for 4.2 miles back to the trailhead parking area. Take three consecutive left forks as you descend the main road parallel to Deadhorse Creek. Unlike the ascent route, your return offers many vistas to the east and south. Finally, cross West Saint Louis Creek and pass a forest trail on the left, which leads back to the trailhead. If you stay on the road, you quickly rise to signs and an intersection. Go left for a few hundred yards and then left again to reach the parking area from which you began.

D.J. Inman at fork with trails to Saint Louis Creek Loop, Deadhorse Creek, and Byers Peak Trailhead.

PHOTO BY DAVE MULLER

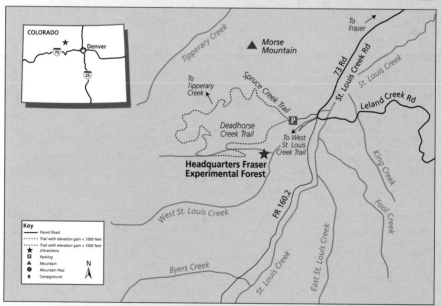

37. Flume Trail

TOUR DISTANCE	2.2 miles each way
TOUR TIME	Out in 46 minutes, back in 54 minutes
STARTING ELEVATION	9,040 feet
HIGHEST ELEVATION	9,040 feet
LOWEST ELEVATION	8,840 feet
ELEVATION GAIN	324 feet (includes 62 extra feet each way)
DIFFICULTY	Easiest
AVALANCHE DANGER	Least
RELEVANT MAPS	Trails Illustrated Number 103 Bottle Pass 7.5 minute Fraser 7.5 minute Grand County Number Four

GETTING THERE: At the traffic light in Fraser on U.S. 40, turn west onto County Road 72. After 0.3 mile, take a right fork that connects with County Road 73 at mile 1.0 from U.S. 40. Turn left here and continue straight up the valley. Avoid the right fork at mile 1.8 and continue on County Road 73 until you park in a large open area on the left at 5.1 miles from U.S. 40.

COMMENT: Here's a short, easy, and pleasant tour through pine forests west of Fraser. The Flume Trail is not open to snowmobiles, but the adjacent Chainsaw Trail is. The Flume Trail runs along the south side of Saint Louis Creek. A west to east route will be described. This starts you at the high point and reaches the lowest part of the Flume Trail at the turnaround point as the Chainsaw Trail is reached.

THE TOUR: Start out to the southeast on the Leland Creek Road (Road 159). Continue 230 yards over snowmobile terrain to a sign on the left for the Flume Trail. Descend this trail to the north over a gentle grade and soon pass through a large open meadow. There are no trail markers between each end of the trail, but this popular route will usually be well tracked. Seventy-five yards before the terminus of this tour there is a great view of Byers Peak. At the end of the Flume Trail, there is a sign and a junction with the Chainsaw Trail. Your return will require some elevation gain and, therefore, will take more time to reach the trailhead on the Leland Creek Road.

SIDEBAR: EXTRA GLOVES

A favorite hand covering for cross-country skiing and snowshoeing is Dachstein mittens, which are made from boiled wool. When it is really cold, you can roll your fingers in a ball in the mitten to warm them. A back-up set of polypro gloves made for cold-weather bicycling are good for warmer days.

Tony Bianchi and D.J. Inman at a rest stop on Flume Trail.

PHOTO BY DAVE MULLER

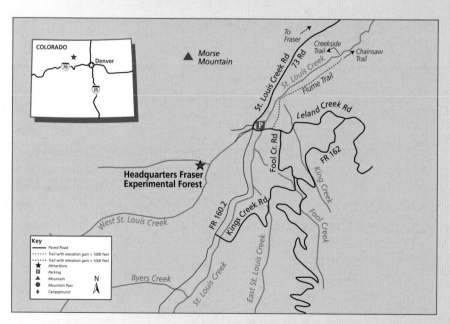

38. Fraser Experimental Forest

TOUR DISTANCE	3 miles each way
TOUR TIME	Out in 76 minutes, back in 63 minutes
STARTING ELEVATION	8,790 feet
HIGHEST ELEVATION	9,070 feet
ELEVATION GAIN	345 feet (includes 65 extra feet)
DIFFICULTY	More difficult
AVALANCHE DANGER	Least
RELEVANT MAPS	Trails Illustrated Number 103 Fraser 7.5 minute Bottle Pass 7.5 minute Grand County Number Four Arapaho National Forest

GETTING THERE: From U.S. 40 in Fraser, turn west at the traffic light on County Road 72 and set your mileage to zero. At mile 0.3 take a right fork and cross a large open area. At mile 1.0 turn left on County Road 73 and continue straight up the valley. Avoid a right fork at mile 1.8. At mile 2.7 park on the right side of County Road 73 at a Travel Restricted Area sign.

COMMENT: This tour through the Fraser Experimental Forest is peaceful and gradual in its elevation changes. Various tree species are encountered. The Fraser Experimental Forest conducts research, which precludes motorized vehicles. Please do not interfere with any equipment in the Fraser Experimental Forest.

THE TOUR: Start out to the west of the Travel Restricted Area sign. Within 50 feet turn left and follow a trail along a series of power poles with two wires above. Just past the seventh pole, take a right (west) fork and within 100 yards pass around a gate and over the Crooked Creek Supply Ditch. After around 1.25 miles of this tour, cross the Big Six Ditch and curve left (south), with the ditch always on your left. Soon reach an open area on the right with several measuring devices. There is a side trail and a bridge to your left. Continue straight (south) and eventually reach an area with many aspen trees. At the upper end of this aspen stand there is a fence to the right of the trail. Proceed to the high point of this tour and then descend to a closed gate at the edge of a large meadow. Follow the trail as it curves left through this clearing and leads to a sturdy wood fence, with the power lines and County Road 73 just beyond. This is a good terminus. Take a break before retracing the route through the lovely forest back to the starting point.

Please be careful to not interfere with any of the instrumentation in the Fraser Experimental Forest.

PHOTO BY DAVE MULLER

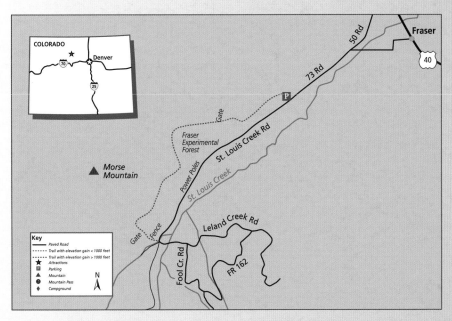

39. Jim Creek

TOUR DISTANCE	2.5 miles each way
TOUR TIME	Up in 70 minutes, down in 40 minutes
STARTING ELEVATION	9,220 feet
HIGHEST ELEVATION	10,075 feet
ELEVATION GAIN	965 feet (includes 55 extra feet each way)
DIFFICULTY	More difficult
AVALANCHE DANGER	Least
RELEVANT MAPS	Trails Illustrated Number 103
	Fraser 7.5 minute
	East Portal 7.5 minute
	Grand County Number Four
	Arapaho National Forest

GETTING THERE: From U.S. 40 at the southern edge of Winter Park, drive into the open area across from the entrance to the Winter Park Ski Area and park near the trailhead signboard close to the large Bonfils Stanton Outdoor Center sign.

COMMENT: One of the more popular snowshoe and cross-country ski tours in Winter Park, this trail ascends along Jim Creek. It begins with a gradual ascent and becomes steeper the farther you go. As you rise up the valley, first a shoulder and then the summit of James Peak comes into view.

THE TOUR: Start out to the south southeast from the trailhead signboard on the Discovery Trail, which takes you over a boardwalk to a trail fork. Go left here and gradually ascend. Pass under a large water pipe and reach a four-way intersection and an aqueduct on Jim Creek after 0.7 mile from the trailhead. Continue straight (southwest) past a sign and ascend the valley with Jim Creek always on the left. At 2.2 miles you will reach an Adopt-A-Trail sign on a wooden pole in a clearing. Continue straight on a steeper trail 0.3 mile to where the trail becomes extremely steep as it curves to the right. Jim Creek and several large boulders will be visible down on the left. This is a good terminus. Take a break before a pleasant return.

SIDEBAR: HOW MUCH GEAR IS TOO MUCH GEAR?

In the backcountry we see some skiers with just a water bottle on a belt and others with "expedition" packs, all on the same out-and-back day trip. We think that a water bottle alone is somewhat minimalist, but these folks appear to be in good shape and out for exercise. We recommend a pack and the Ten Essentials that we describe individually as sidebars. We also recommend common sense. In other words, on a bright sunny day, we think that stuffing an expedition parka made of down in your pack is overkill, but a down vest is probably a worthwhile addition.

Skiers making their way up Jim Creek.

PHOTO BY DAVE MULLER

PHOTO BY JAY FELL

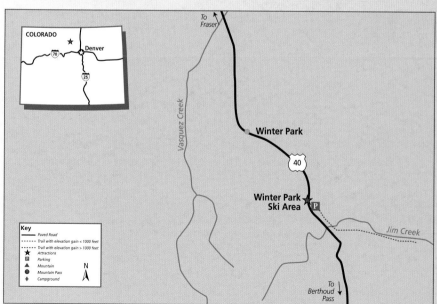

91

40. King Creek

TOUR DISTANCE	5.3 miles each way
TOUR TIME	Out in 170 minutes, back in 139 minutes
STARTING ELEVATION	9,032 feet
HIGHEST ELEVATION	9,485 feet
ELEVATION GAIN	834 feet (includes 381 extra feet)
DIFFICULTY	More difficult
AVALANCHE DANGER	Least
RELEVANT MAPS	Trails Illustrated Number 103 Fraser 7.5 minute Bottle Pass 7.5 minute Grand County Number Four Arapaho National Forest

GETTING THERE: From U.S. 40 at the traffic light in Fraser turn west on County Road 72 and set your mileage to zero. After 0.4 mile take the right fork and drive through a vast meadow. At 1 mile turn left on to County Road 73 and continue straight up the valley on the wide Saint Louis Creek Road. Avoid the road on the right at 1.8 miles. Park in the clearing on the left at 5.2 miles and the Leland Creek Road, just before the junction.

COMMENT: The Winter Park and Fraser area is blessed with abundant snowfall and many trails. Some of the best trails lie within the Fraser Experimental Forest where snowmobiles, except for forest maintenance, are forbidden. The King Creek Trail is a long, lovely trek on wide roads through the forest, with intermittent views of the high peaks to the west and north. The far point is the Leland Creek Road or Aqueduct Road at the northern edge of the Fraser Experimental Forest.

THE TOUR: From the parking area, go northeast 0.4 mile until you reach FR 160.2 and the turn right heading south. After 1.5 miles from the starting point, you will reach signs and an intersection. Continue up to the left (east) on the King Creek Road. After an ascent, the trail winds through the forest on fairly level terrain before descending a few hundred yards and then rising steeply in an open area before again reaching level terrain. Eventually you reach a sign and a four-way intersection at mile 3.5 of your outgoing route. Take the second road on the right, which is the continuation of the King Creek Road. This final segment rises and falls en route to a road barrier and the Leland Creek Road. This is the turnaround point and allows you to avoid snowmobiles on the Leland Creek Road. There are good views of Byers Peak, Bills Peak, and Bottle Peak along the way.

King Creek Trail with Battle Mountain in the background.

PHOTO BY DAVE MULLER

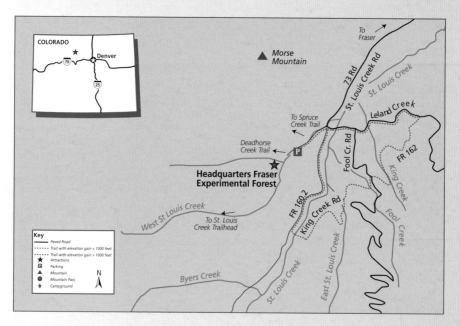

41. Monarch Lake Loop

TOUR DISTANCE	5.8 miles (total loop)
TOUR TIME	195 minutes
STARTING ELEVATION	8,340 feet
HIGHEST ELEVATION	8,361 feet
ELEVATION GAIN	721 feet (includes 700 extra feet)
DIFFICULTY	More difficult
AVALANCHE DANGER	Least
RELEVANT MAPS	Trails Illustrated Number 102
	Monarch Lake 7.5 minute
	Grand County Number Two
	Arapaho National Forest

GETTING THERE: From U.S. 40 on the western edge of Granby, drive north on U.S. 34 for 5.4 miles. Turn right on County Road 6 and drive on the good main road for another 8.5 miles. Park near the barrier on County Road 6 just past a four-way intersection.

COMMENT: The trail around Monarch Lake provides a good outing during the entire year. Hiking in the warmer weather and snowshoeing or cross-country skiing when snow covers the trail are all enjoyable. Because there are intermittent rocks and sometimes fallen trees on the occasionally narrow trail, snowshoes are recommended for a winter outing, but nordic skis are also workable. Monarch Lake is a constructed reservoir that collects water from Buchanan and Arapahoe Creeks. Because most of the loop lies within the Indian Peaks Wilderness, vehicles are forbidden, and dogs must be kept on a leash.

THE TOUR: Begin up the road from the barrier to the north northeast. After almost a mile, pass around a second barrier and quickly reach a cabin and trail register on the right just before signs at Monarch Lake. Continue on the Cascade Trail to the east along the left side of the lake. After 1.8 miles, enter the Indian Peaks Wilderness at the signs. Another 0.7 mile brings you to a signed fork. Continue to the right (southwest) on the Arapaho Spur Trail and soon cross a bridge over the Buchanan Creek. The trail rises and falls another 0.7 mile to another bridge over Arapaho Creek. A trail on the left just before this bridge leads to Arapaho Pass. Continue straight past a cabin ruin on the left and soon leave the Wilderness Area. Monarch Lake will come into view through the trees on the right. Eventually pass a large mining artifact as the trail leads back to the beginning of the loop, after passing over the outlet of the lake. Retrace your route down the road on the left.

Monarch Lake looking east toward the Indian Peaks.

PHOTO BY DAVE MULLER

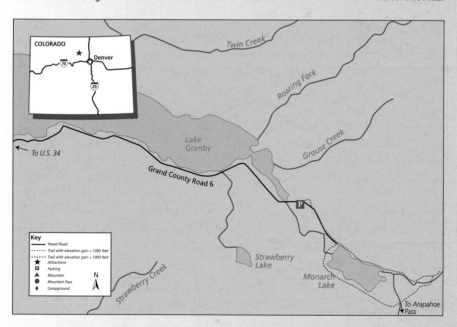

42. Saint Louis Creek Loop

TOUR DISTANCE	Up in 4.6 miles, down in 2.2 miles
TOUR TIME	Up in 127 minutes, down in 40 minutes
STARTING ELEVATION	9,060 feet
HIGHEST ELEVATION	9,514 feet
ELEVATION GAIN	539 feet (includes 85 extra feet)
DIFFICULTY	More difficult
AVALANCHE DANGER	Least
RELEVANT MAPS	Trails Illustrated Number 103 Bottle Pass 7.5 minute Grand County Number Four Arapaho National Forest

GETTING THERE: From the traffic light in the town of Fraser, drive north on U.S. 40 for 0.2 mile and turn left onto Eisenhower Drive. Set your mileage to zero. Cross the railroad tracks and make an immediate left turn. Follow this road, curving to the right, and ascend the valley on County Road 73. Pass the Saint Louis Campground on the left at 2.8 miles. You reach a four-way intersection at 4.7 miles. Park anywhere on the right in an extensive parking area.

COMMENT: Traversing a loop on foot provides different scenery and gradients, depending on whether you pursue a clockwise or counterclockwise direction. This clockwise route description of the Saint Louis Creek Loop is less frequently chosen by nordic skiers or snowshoers but is equally enjoyable.

THE TOUR: Begin your tour to the east on the road into the parking area and turn right (south) on County Road 73, the Saint Louis Creek Road. Within 200 yards, proceed around a road barrier and continue up the wide road for 1.5 miles to a four-way intersection. The King Creek Road rises on the left and a steep shortcut of the Saint Louis Creek Loop rises on the right. Continue straight (south) on the wide road for 1 mile to a sign and road junction, after passing the Byers Peak Campground on the left. Proceed north on the road to the right and join a level road that continues a meandering 2.2 miles to reach an intersection. The road on the left ascends to the Byers Peak Trailhead. You, however, descend to the right (east) another 2.2 miles to the trailhead parking area to complete the loop. En route, you cross West Saint Louis Creek, continue straight past the Deadhorse Creek Road on the left, and take a final left fork back to the trailhead. You have completed a 6.8-mile circuit.

TOP: Saint Louis Creek Loop.

PHOTOS BY DAVE MULLER

BOTTOM: Trailhead for Saint Louis Creek Loop and Deadhorse Creek Loop.

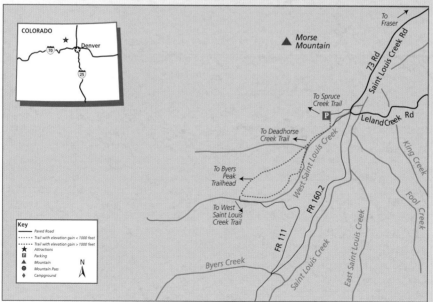

Key
— Paved Road
••••• Trail with elevation gain < 1000 feet
••••• Trail with elevation gain > 1000 feet
★ Attractions
P Parking
▲ Mountain
◉ Mountain Pass
◆ Campground

43. Saint Louis Lake Trailhead

TOUR DISTANCE	4.1 miles each way
TOUR TIME	Up in 120 minutes, down in 92 minutes
STARTING ELEVATION	9,070 feet
HIGHEST ELEVATION	9,500 feet
ELEVATION GAIN	510 feet (includes 40 extra feet each way)
DIFFICULTY	Easiest
AVALANCHE DANGER	Least
RELEVANT MAPS	Trails Illustrated Number 103 Bottle Pass 7.5 minute Byers Peak 7.5 minute Grand County Number Four

GETTING THERE: From U.S. 40 at the traffic light in Fraser, drive west on County Road 72 for 0.3 mile. Turn right at the intersection and cross open terrain for 0.8 mile until you reach County Road 73. Turn left and proceed straight up the valley on the main road for 4.7 miles to a road barrier beyond a four-way intersection. Park on the right at the Fraser Experimental Forest Headquarters.

COMMENT: A good cross-country ski tour requires adequate snow depth, a gentle grade, a wide trail, and several intermediate destinations. The road to the Saint Louis Lake Trailhead, west of Fraser in the Fraser Experimental Forest, meets these criteria. Please do not interfere with any equipment in the Fraser Experimental Forest.

THE TOUR: Begin skiing south up the road through the trees. After 1.25 miles, continue straight at the four-way intersection. The King Creek Road leads to the left and a steep section that connects to the Saint Louis Loop ascends to the right. Pass a side road on the left to the Byers Creek Campground after another 0.7 mile. The road then ascends a gentle grade to a signed fork. The road to the Byers Peak Trailhead and the Saint Louis Creek Loop proceeds to the right. Continue straight and quickly pass another connecting road to the right. You have now come more than 2 miles. Some may wish to turn back here or pursue the routes up the right fork. As you continue south up the valley, the terrain opens up more and Saint Louis Peak can be seen to the south southeast. At 4 miles, you reach a road junction at a clearing. The left fork ends quickly at an aqueduct and green utility hut. Continue straight up the main road for another 0.1 mile to a signboard at the summer trailhead for Saint Louis Lake. Give yourself a break before the gradual descent back to your starting point on the wide road.

Frank Beghter at Saint Louis Creek Trailhead.   PHOTO BY DAVE MULLER

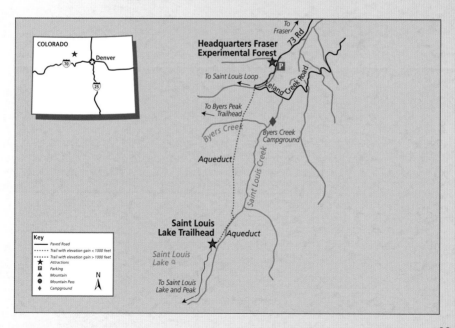

44. Highline Trail

TOUR DISTANCE	3 miles each way
TOUR TIME	Up in 120 minutes, down in 74 minutes
STARTING ELEVATION	9,625 feet
HIGHEST ELEVATION	10,960 feet
ELEVATION GAIN	1,575 feet (includes 120 extra feet each way)
DIFFICULTY	More difficult
AVALANCHE DANGER	Least
RELEVANT MAPS	Trails Illustrated Number 127
	Mount Massive 7.5 minute
	Lake County
	San Isabel National Forest

GETTING THERE: From the intersection at 6th Street in central Leadville, drive south on U.S. 24 for 3.9 miles and turn right onto Colorado 300. Follow this paved road 2.3 miles and turn left into the National Fish Hatchery. Drive 0.1 mile into the complex and park near the trailhead on the left.

COMMENT: Not many nordic skiers or snowshoers use the fine trails of the National Fish Hatchery southwest of Leadville at the foot of Mount Massive. Snowmobiles are forbidden. At the halfway point of this tour, you enter the Mount Massive Wilderness. There are several connecting trails in this area. The Highline Trail is the most demanding. In the early stages of your ascent, you pass the site of the Evergreen Lakes Hotel, which hosted the famous Molly Brown's wedding breakfast and burned to the ground in January 1894.

THE TOUR: Start on foot up the road to the southeast. Blue tree blazes will guide you. Within a few hundred yards, take a right fork and ascend to another fork at the Evergreen Lakes Hotel site on the right. Keep right at this fork and always keep the lakes to your left. After 0.6 mile, continue straight (south southeast) at the prominent intersection. (The trail ascending on the right will parallel Rock Creek to the Colorado Trail). The trail soon ascends a steep stretch past a pond on the left. At the fork and a fishing catch-and-release sign, go left (southwest). Another 0.5 mile brings you past the wilderness boundary. There follow several steep sections (the steepest being the last few hundred yards) to reach the Colorado Trail. Climbing skins are advised for the skier. At the Colorado Trail, which runs to the left and right, there are signs and a continuation of the Highline Trail to Native Lake straight ahead. Rest and refresh before the steep return back.

Trailhead sign for Highline Trail.

PHOTO BY DAVID HITE

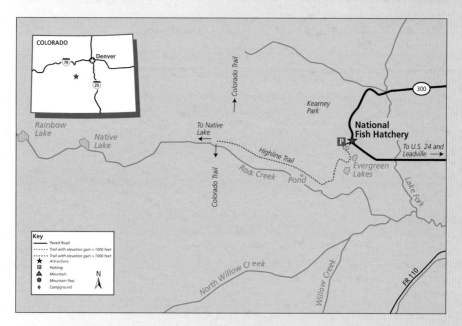

45. Interlaken

TOUR DISTANCE	2.7 miles each way
TOUR TIME	Out in 75 minutes, back in 67 minutes
STARTING ELEVATION	9,200 feet
HIGHEST ELEVATION	9,220 feet
ELEVATION GAIN	120 feet (includes 50 extra feet each way)
DIFFICULTY	Easiest
AVALANCHE DANGER	Least
RELEVANT MAPS	Trails Illustrated Number 110 Granite 7.5 minute Lake County San Isabel National Forest

GETTING THERE: From East 6th Street in Leadville, drive south on Harrison Avenue (which is U.S. 24). After 15.1 miles on U.S. 24, turn right (west) on Colorado 82. After 0.8 miles on Colorado 82, turn left onto a dirt road opposite a wooden cabin. Follow this road 0.4 mile and go left at the fork. After another 0.2 mile, park at the end of the plowed area near some signs.

COMMENT: The Twin Lakes area between Leadville and Buena Vista is very scenic. In addition to the lakes, some of Colorado's highest peaks loom above to the west. This ski and showshoe tour puts you in the center of this paradise. As you ski west on the Colorado Trail along the edge of the lake, you face Mount Elbert, Colorado's highest mountain, en route to the ghost town of Interlaken. Built as a resort in the 1870s between the Twin Lakes, Interlaken is now merely remnants.

THE TOUR: Begin south southwest from the parking area on a road. Continue 20 yards past the sign that forbids overnight camping, turn right, and proceed west toward a fence with Mount Elbert in the background. Follow the Colorado Trail signs along the southern edge of the lake until you finally reach the former Interlaken town site just before the isthmus between the two lakes. Enjoy the beautiful surroundings before your return. Stay off the lake because the ice may be too thin.

SIDEBAR: THE INTERLAKEN HOTEL

Construction of the Interlaken Hotel complex began in 1879 and was expanded after James V. Dexter bought the lakeside resort and grounds in 1883. The resort had some of the best facilities for its time, including comfortable rooms with a view of the forest and lakes. The resort also had a log tavern, pool hall, and sheds to accommodate guests and their horses, plus a unique six-sided privy with a separate room and door for each side reserved for guests in the hotel.

The view across Twin Lakes to Interlaken.

PHOTO BY DAVE MULLER

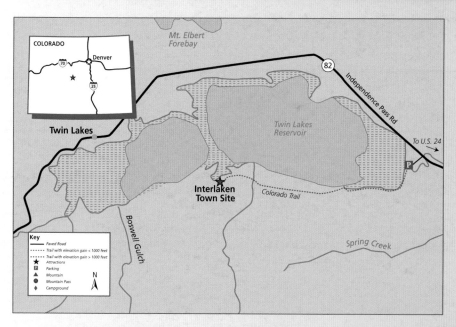

46. Kearney Park Loop

TOUR DISTANCE	5.9 miles (total loop)
TOUR TIME	Out in 110 minutes, back in 58 minutes
STARTING ELEVATION	9,620 feet
HIGHEST ELEVATION	10,665 feet
ELEVATION GAIN	1,305 feet (includes 260 extra feet)
DIFFICULTY	Most difficult
AVALANCHE DANGER	Least
RELEVANT MAPS	Trails Illustrated Number 127
	Mount Massive 7.5 minute
	Lake County
	San Isabel National Forest

GETTING THERE: From 6th Street in central Leadville drive south on U.S. 24 for 3.9 miles and turn right onto Colorado 300. Follow this road for 2.3 miles and turn left into the National Fish Hatchery. Drive up the main road for 0.2 miles and park at the trailhead on the left across from the visitor center.

COMMENT: There are two tour possibilities on the hatchery grounds. This one to Kearney Park is the more difficult with some steep ascents. The other leads to the Colorado Trail. I would advise waiting for fresh snow before trying these tours.

THE TOUR: Begin southeast up the road from the trail register. Within 100 yards take a right fork and pass one of the six Evergreen Lakes on your left. After another 150 yards, take the right fork at the sign commemorating the former site of the Evergreen Lakes Hotel. Another 20 yards brings you to another fork, and again you ski to the right. Blue diamond signs on the trees mark the trail for this entire loop. Keep right again at another fork 0.5 mile past the last one. Continue west with Rock Creek on your left. Good views of Mount Massive to the southwest occur at intervals along this route. Pass the boundary of the Mount Massive Wilderness and some signs until you reach a junction with the Colorado Trail 3 miles from the trailhead. (If you retrace the trail from here back to the trailhead, the difficulty of the tour is considerably less.) To continue the loop, ascend steeply to the right (west northwest). The next mile is a steep ascent into Kearney Park at the highest elevation of this loop. Take the right fork at the eastern edge of Kearney Park and leave the Colorado Trail. The next 2 miles provide many thrills and chills on the rapid descent back to Colorado 300. Carry your skis or snowshoes to the right a few hundred yards on the road down to the fish hatchery and the trailhead from which you started.

Northern trailhead to Kearney Park Loop.

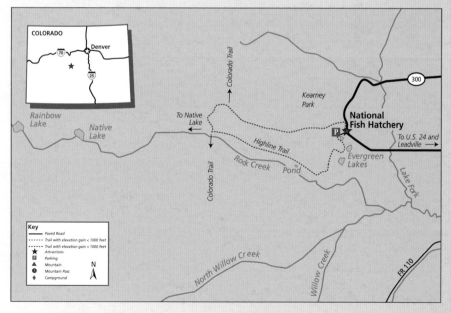

47. Lily Lake Loop

TOUR DISTANCE	Up to lake in 3.3 miles, down in 1.9 miles
TOUR TIME	Up in 85 minutes, down in 32 minutes
STARTING ELEVATION	10,310 feet
HIGHEST ELEVATION	10,680 feet
ELEVATION GAIN	685 feet (includes 315 extra feet)
DIFFICULTY	More difficult
AVALANCHE DANGER	Least
RELEVANT MAPS	Trails Illustrated Number 109 Leadville North 7.5 minute Lake County San Isabel National Forest

GETTING THERE: At the northern edge of Leadville, from Colorado 91, take U.S. 24 and drive northwest for 7 miles. Then turn left at Crane Park and follow this plowed road for 1.3 miles. Park on the left with the trailhead on the right. (When icy, this road can be difficult.)

COMMENT: Many Nordic ski and snowshoe trails can be found northeast of Leadville near Tennessee Pass and the Continental Divide. One of these is the Lily Lake Loop, which uses part of the Colorado Trail. The trail is well marked by blue diamond signs on the trees. A clockwise route will be described here, but you can readily make the loop in the opposite direction.

THE TOUR: Begin to the west northwest from the road into a large meadow and quickly pass a cabin on the right. Keep straight on the main trail, enter the trees, and continue to a sign and four-way intersection after 0.5 mile. For the clockwise loop, take the Colorado Trail on the left (west northwest). Follow the blue diamonds up the West Tennessee Creek Valley until you reach another sign and intersection at 0.9 mile of your tour. Leave the Colorado Trail and ascend the right fork to the west northwest. A gradual 1 mile further brings you to a steep ascent of several hundred feet to the north before you reach the high point of the loop in the trees. Lily Lake is below but not yet visible. Never leave the blue diamond marked trail. Descend steeply to the lake as the trail takes you over and around some fallen timber. Rest and refresh at the rim of the circular lake before passing around it, either to your left or right. Continue to a sign near a blocked road on the north side of the lake and then follow the wide trail to the right (east). Descend back to the four-way intersection, which began the loop, and continue straight back to the trailhead.

TOP: Near the trailhead to Lily Lake Loop.   PHOTO BY DAVE MULLER

BOTTOM: Homestake Peak above Lily Lake Loop.   PHOTO BY TERRY ROOT

48. Mitchell Creek Loop

TOUR DISTANCE	7.3 miles (total loop)
TOUR TIME	Out in 95 minutes, back in 75 minutes
STARTING ELEVATION	10,424 feet
HIGHEST ELEVATION	10,600 feet
ELEVATION GAIN	860 feet (includes 684 extra feet)
DIFFICULTY	More difficult
AVALANCHE DANGER	Least
RELEVANT MAPS	Trails Illustrated Number 109 Leadville North 7.5 minute Pando 7.5 minute Colorado Trail Map Number Eight Eagle County Number Four Lake County

GETTING THERE: Take U.S. 24 to Tennessee Pass north of Leadville and south of Minturn. Park in the designated area on the west side of the pass.

COMMENT: The Mitchell Creek Loop begins and ends at Tennessee Pass on the Continental Divide. It can be traveled in either direction and uses part of the Colorado Trail. A counterclockwise route will be described here. Blue diamond symbols mark the trail well and occasionally state the distance you have covered. This is one of the better Colorado cross-country ski and snowshoe outings.

THE TOUR: Begin to the northwest past the trail sign on an old railroad bed that is part of the Colorado Trail. Pass a trail to the Powderhound Loop on the left and an old stone kiln on the left within 500 yards of the trailhead. Stay on the main trail as it descends to the west. Pass another Powderhound Loop trail on the left. Keep left at 1.5 miles as the Colorado Trail continues down to the right. It will be another 0.7 mile to Mitchell Creek and the lowest point of this tour. From the creek crossing, ascend gradually to the southwest. Pass around a fallen tree, continue to a level clearing, and progress upward to the highest elevation of this trek. You are now at a utility cabin and the aqueduct known as Wurts Ditch, on the Continental Divide and the boundary between Lake and Eagle Counties. Cross the bridge and descend south on the Wurts Ditch Road. Trek 0.5 mile below the bridge, and go left at the signed intersection onto the Colorado Trail. Follow the blue diamond markers on the narrow trail as it rises and falls through the trees. A mile before the parking area, you pass a trail to the Treeline Loop on your left. Keep right and continue up to the ridge, and then quickly descend to a trailhead sign at the eastern side of the parking area and the end of your loop tour.

Clockwise trailhead to Mitchell Creek Loop.

PHOTO BY DAVE MULLER

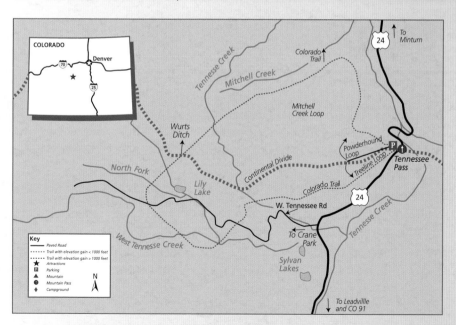

109

49. Old Railroad Run

TOUR DISTANCE	2.5 miles each way
TOURING TIME	Out in 50 minutes, back in 60 minutes
STARTING ELEVATION	10,424 feet
HIGHEST ELEVATION	10,424 feet (Tennessee Pass)
LOWEST ELEVATION	10,100 feet
ELEVATION GAIN	334 feet (includes an extra 5 feet each way)
DIFFICULTY	Easiest
AVALANCHE DANGER	Least
RELEVANT MAPS	Trails Illustrated Number 109 Leadville North 7.5 minute Pando 7.5 minute Eagle County Number Four

GETTING THERE: From the junction of Colorado 91 and U.S. 24 north of Leadville, drive northwest on U.S. 24 for 8.6 miles to Tennessee Pass. Park in the designated area on the left at the pass (opposite the road to Ski Cooper).

COMMENT: This modest tour utilizes a segment of the Colorado Trail and an old railroad bed. The grade is very gentle. The adjacent downhill slopes of Ski Cooper and its nordic center make this a good outing for families or groups with both downhill and cross-country skiers, as well as snowshoers. Any cross-country ski route can also be traversed with snowshoes.

THE TOUR: Begin west northwest from the Colorado Trail sign on the west side of Tennessee Pass. After 0.5 mile, keep right as you pass a kiln remnant on the left. Colorado Trail signs will appear at intervals. After another 1.7 miles, the Colorado Trail forks to the right. Keep left on the railroad bed and continue another 0.7 mile to the end point of the tour; you will see a Mitchell Loop trail sign on a tree to the left with an open valley to your right. Galena Mountain and Homestake Peak are visible to the west southwest. Ascend back to Tennessee Pass by retracing your path. As you approach the pass, the ski slopes on Cooper Hill can be seen straight ahead.

SIDEBAR: COMPASS AND MAP

You are above the tree line on a frozen lake and a 30 mile-per-hour wind brings in a front and a whiteout. What to do? Take out your compass and determine your heading. To retreat turn around 180 degrees. Now take out your map (hang on to it in the wind) and with your new compass bearing, plot a course back to the trail and eventually the trailhead. You do have a compass and map, don't you? You don't? No worries. Whiteouts are usually over in a couple of cold, brutal hours.

Homestake Peak from Old Railroad Run.

PHOTO BY DAVE MULLER

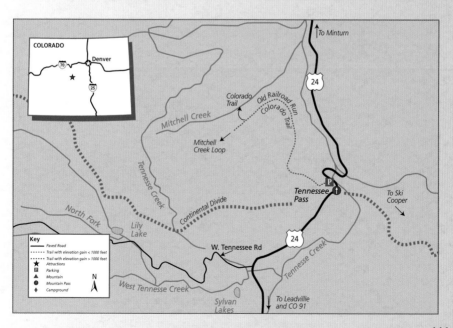

111

50. Powderhound Loop

TOUR DISTANCE	2.6 miles (total loop)
TOUR TIME	Up in 45 minutes, down in 30 minutes
STARTING ELEVATION	10,424 feet (Tennessee Pass)
HIGHEST ELEVATION	10,660 feet
ELEVATION GAIN	266 feet (includes 30 extra feet)
DIFFICULTY	More difficult
AVALANCHE DANGER	Least
RELEVANT MAPS	Trails Illustrated Number 109 Leadville North 7.5 minute Lake County White River National Forest

GETTING THERE: Take U.S. 24 to Tennessee Pass between Leadville and Minturn. Park in the lot on the west side of the road at the pass (across from the entrance to Ski Cooper). If this lot is not plowed, park nearby off the road.

COMMENT: There are twin loop trails for skiers and snowshoers west of Tennessee Pass. These are the Powderhound Loop and the Treeline Loop. Both have connections with the Continental Divide and the Colorado Trail. The more northerly loop is the Powderhound. In my opinion, the best way to traverse it is in the clockwise direction. The trail is well marked, and snow is usually abundant during the winter months.

THE TOUR: Begin west northwest from the parking area, pass several signs, and, within 300 yards, take the left fork at a sign and ascend into the trees. Blue diamond signs on the trees mark the route. (If you are breaking trail, finding these markers can be an enjoyable challenge.) After a steep mile you will reach the high point of this tour at a sign in a sparsely wooded flat area. Turn right (north) here and descend a mile following the blue diamonds to a sign at an intersection with the Old Railroad Run, which is also part of the Colorado Trail. Turn right here and gently ascend back toward Ski Cooper and the trailhead.

SIDEBAR: FIRE STARTER

On the rare occasion that you have to build a fire in the winter, there will be a good reason for it. Either you are lost and need a fire to get you through the night, someone in the party is sick or injured and needs the warmth until help arrives, or you are winter camping, which is its own form of lunacy. We've found that tearing pages out of a guidebook and using them as tinder for twigs isn't nearly as good as having several balls of sawdust and wax that light easily and give off a sustained flame for long enough to get a decent fire started.

Trail marker for Powderhound Loop.

PHOTO BY DAVE MULLER

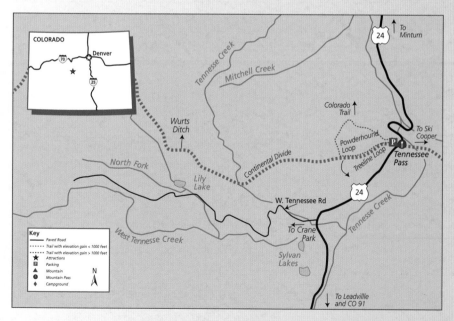

51. Tenth Mountain Division Hut

TOUR TIME	4.8 miles each way
TOUR DISTANCE	Up in 130 minutes, down in 110 minutes
STARTING ELEVATION	10,137 feet (Crane Park Trailhead)
HIGHEST ELEVATION	11,370 feet
ELEVATION GAIN	1,683 feet (includes 225 extra feet each way)
DIFFICULTY	More difficult
AVALANCHE DANGER	Moderate
RELEVANT MAPS	Trails Illustrated Numbers 109 and 126 Homestake Reservoir 7.5 minute Leadville North 7.5 minute Tenth Mountain Hut Association Map Lake County San Isabel National Forest

GETTING THERE: From the intersection of Colorado 91 and U.S. 24 at the north edge of Leadville, drive northwest on U.S. 24 for 7.1 miles and turn left onto a side road. Park within 100 yards near a trail sign on the right. This is the Crane Park Trailhead. If the road is plowed and passable, you may be able to drive 0.9 miles farther and park on the right. The data for this ski tour, however, is based on beginning from the Crane Park Trailhead.

COMMENT: The huts of the Tenth Mountain Division Hut Association can be rented for overnight use (phone 970-925-5775). They also make good destinations for intermediate day ski tours. The Tenth Mountain Division Hut was built in 1989 and lies in a meadow east of Homestake Peak. Do not disturb hut renters.

THE TOUR: Start west southwest up the road, which may be quite icy. After 1 mile, keep left and continue past a parking area and a trailhead on the right. Descend the road another 0.2 mile and take the right fork at the sign directing you toward the Colorado Trail. You are now proceeding west northwest on Road 131. Pass a cabin on the right, and 0.5 mile from the last fork, keep straight at the four-way intersection and some signs. Follow the blue diamond markers on the trees. Ascend through the trees and keep straight for a few hundred yards as a trail enters from the left. After another mile you reach a fork just below Lily Lake. (The straight route reaches Lily Lake on the left within 100 yards.) To reach the hut, take the right (northwest) fork, descend slightly across a drainage area, and then ascend more steeply by trail through the trees. More open areas are traversed as you go higher in the basin. The final part of the trail curves to the right (north), and the hut comes into view as you reach a final ridge with Homestake Peak to your left.

Tenth Mountain Division Hut.

PHOTO BY DAVE MULLER

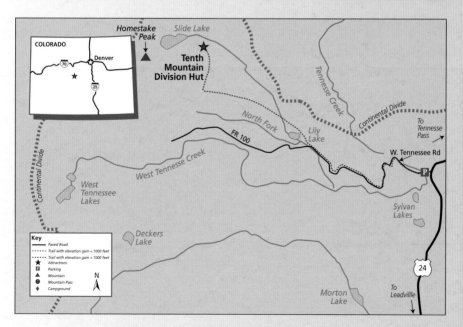

52. Treeline Loop

TOUR DISTANCE	2.4 miles (total loop)
TOUR TIME	Up in 45 minutes, down in 50 minutes
STARTING ELEVATIONS	10,424 feet
HIGHEST ELEVATION	10,660 feet
ELEVATION GAIN	566 feet (includes 330 extra feet)
DIFFICULTY	More difficult
AVALANCHE DANGER	Least
RELEVANT MAPS	Trails Illustrated Number 109 Leadville North 7.5 minute Lake County San Isabel National Forest

GETTING THERE: Take U.S. 24 to Tennessee Pass between Leadville and Minturn. Park in the lot on the west side of the road at the pass (across from Ski Cooper). Tennessee Pass lies 8.7 miles from the junction of U.S. 24 and Colorado 91 north of Leadville.

COMMENT: Around Tennessee Pass there is a wide selection of ski tours. A shorter tour is the Treeline Loop, which uses both the Colorado Trail and the Continental Divide as it follows blue diamond signs on the trees. This tour will be described in a counterclockwise direction, but it can readily be traveled in the opposite way. Another possibility is to combine this route with the adjacent Powderhound Loop to the north. Always stay connected to the blue diamond markers.

THE TOUR: From the parking area, begin west northwest by trail past several signs. Within 300 yards, take a left fork onto the Treeline Loop and the Continental Divide at a sign and ascend into the trees. From this point no snowmobiles are allowed. After a moderately steep mile, you reach the high point of this tour on a mesa and a sign. The Powderhound Loop leads to the north. You proceed southwest (left) on the Treeline Loop and follow the blue diamonds down through the forest. After 0.3 mile from the high point, you will reach a junction with the Colorado Trail. Turn left (southeast) and ascend the final mile back to the parking area.

SIDEBAR: MOONCRUISING

Most of us have a favorite quiet winter trail that we know almost as well as we know our own neighborhood route for jogging or walking the dog. On a clear, cold night during a full or near-full moon, take this favorite backcountry trail for a snowshoe or cross-country ski. It will be so bright out that you won't need a headlamp, but take one anyhow. You'll be amazed at how beautiful your trail is in the moonlight.

Jackie Muller at the junction of Treeline Loop and Powderhound Loop.

PHOTO BY DAVE MULLER

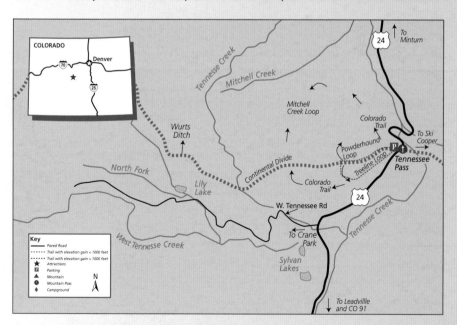

117

53. Vance's Cabin

TOUR DISTANCE	2.9 miles each way
TOUR TIME	Up in 80 minutes, down in 64 minutes
STARTING ELEVATION	10,550 feet
HIGHEST ELEVATION	11,120 feet (top of meadow above the cabin)
ELEVATION GAIN	1,040 feet (includes 470 extra feet)
DIFFICULTY	More difficult
AVALANCHE DANGER	Least
RELEVANT MAPS	Trails Illustrated Number 109 Leadville North 7.5 minute Pando 7.5 minute Tenth Mountain Division Hut System—Chicago Ridge

GETTING THERE: Take U.S. 24 to Tennessee Pass between Leadville and Colorado 91 to the south and Minturn and Interstate 70 to the north. Drive west 0.5 mile into the Ski Cooper complex and park near the Nordic Center or on the left.

COMMENT: Vance's Cabin is one of many mountain huts that can be privately rented both in winter and summer. (Call the Tenth Mountain Division Hut Association at 970-925-5775 for details.) Located north of Ski Cooper near Tennessee Pass, the hut makes a good destination with a great panorama of high peaks to the south and southwest. As with all of these huts, stay out unless you have reserved space for yourself. Keep some distance from the huts and respect the privacy of those who have made reservations.

THE TOUR: Start northeast down the road opposite the Nordic Center. Proceed 0.5 mile parallel to the creek, and then take the left fork and cross the creek at a barrier. Follow the trail north northwest up into the trees. After another 0.4 mile, you will enter an open area. Avoid the valley to the northeast and follow the left trail as it steepens and continues generally to the north. Widely spaced blue diamond markers and pink ribbons on the trees help define the route. At the upper edge of the clearing, you have come 1.1 miles from the trailhead. After another 1.5 miles through the trees, you reach a large open burn area just past the highest elevation of this tour. Follow the markers and trail west down the 0.25-mile trek through some burnt stumps to the large three-level cabin on your left at the edge of the forest. The large open area before and above Vance's Cabin provides good free skiing and snowshoeing opportunities. Taylor Hill to the east northeast offers an open summit with spectacular scenery. From here Mount Elbert can be seen to the south and Mount Massive to the southwest. Be careful to find and retrace your route back.

Ski Cooper in the background from Vance's Cabin.

PHOTO BY DAVE MULLER

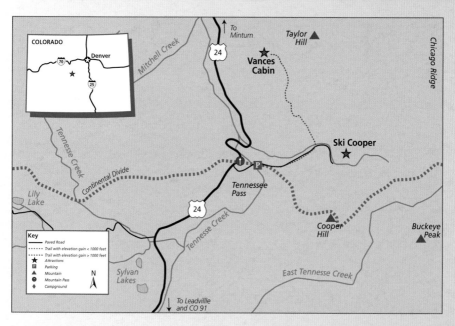

54. Bruce's Trail

TOUR DISTANCE	3.3 miles (total loop)
TOUR TIME	60 minutes
STARTING ELEVATION	9,200 feet
HIGHEST ELEVATION	9,300 feet
ELEVATION GAIN	380 feet (includes 280 extra feet)
DIFFICULTY	More difficult
AVALANCHE DANGER	Least
RELEVANT MAPS	Trails Illustrated Number 118 Mount Werner 7.5 minute Routt County Number Four Routt National Forest

GETTING THERE: Take U.S. 40 to Rabbit Ears Pass, which is southeast of Steamboat Springs and northwest of Kremmling. From the east summit of the pass, drive west 6 miles and park on the right (north) near the large trailhead sign. From the west summit, drive east 1.6 miles and park on the left.

COMMENT: The winter recreational opportunities of wonderful Rabbit Ears Pass have been increased by the addition of Bruce's Trail. The trail is intended only for cross-country skiers and snowshoers in the winter. (Bikers and hikers are welcome in the summer). Bruce's Trail was established by volunteers of the Northwest Colorado Nordic Council to honor Bruce Albin, an outdoor enthusiast, who died in 1992. It consists of two connecting loops that are traveled in a counterclockwise direction. The upper loop is easier than the lower. A trail map at the trailhead clarifies the route. Dogs and motor vehicles are forbidden.

THE TOUR: Begin north, parallel to the road, for 30 yards before turning left and approaching the forest to the northwest. Follow the frequently placed blue diamond tree blazes that mark the trail. At the top of a rise, take the right fork and descend along the lower loop. The wide road rises and falls frequently, providing some good but brief ski runs, with Walton Creek below on your right. There are two main connecting trails to the upper loop. To lengthen your tour, take the left fork at the first intersection and the right fork at the second junction encountered on the lower loop. Continue through the evergreen forest to complete the loop and return to the trailhead. You might want to repeat the two loops again if time and energy permit.

Twilight near Bruce's Trail.

PHOTO BY DAVE COOPER

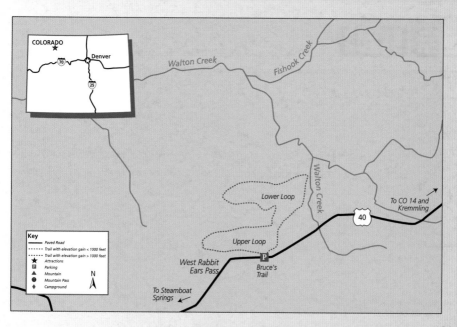

55. Fox Curve Loop

TOUR DISTANCE	3.8 miles (total loop)
TOUR TIME	115 minutes
STARTING ELEVATION	9,420 feet
HIGHEST ELEVATION	9,605 feet
ELEVATION GAIN	910 feet (includes 725 extra feet)
DIFFICULTY	More difficult
AVALANCHE DANGER	Least
RELEVANT MAPS	Trails Illustrated Number 118 Mount Werner 7.5 minute Routt County Number Four Routt National Forest

GETTING THERE: Take U.S. 40 to Rabbit Ears Pass, northwest of Kremmling and southeast of Steamboat Springs. Park in the Fox Curve parking area off the north side of U.S. 40. This parking area lies 4.8 miles west of East Rabbit Ears Pass and 2.8 miles east of West Rabbit Ears Pass.

COMMENT: Here is another treasure for cross-country skiers and snowshoers from the Rabbit Ears Pass area that has lots of ups and downs on a route that is well marked by blue blazes. As is typical for Rabbit Ears Pass, there are several magnificent open meadows along this loop. Rabbit Ears Pass receives good snowfall and offers several loop trails for the winter trekker. It is one of the premier Colorado winter playgrounds.

THE TOUR: From the parking area, begin north to two signboards at the trailhead. Proceed to the left (west) and you will quickly reach a fork with two steeply descending trails. These are the beginning and ending parts of the Fox Curve Loop. The counterclockwise approach starts at the right fork and proceeds down to a crossing of Walton Creek. A large, open basin will be on the left and you will follow a series of blue blazes, some on trees and some on poles, along the right side of the basin. At the northern edge of the clearing, enter the trees and ascend to the high point of this loop at a solitary stump on the right. The trail then drops to the valley floor and another vast, flat basin. Follow the blue markers and curve back to the left, cross a tributary of Walton Creek, and reenter the basin you traversed on the initial segment of the loop. Follow the blue poles to the south. The highway traffic on U.S. 40 can be seen and heard in the distance. The tower atop North Walton Peak may be visible to the south southeast. At the end of the basin, curve left and ascend some steep slopes to the terminus of the loop and the trailhead signs.

Trailhead sign for the snowmobile-free trails west of Rabbit Ears Pass.

PHOTO BY DAVE MULLER

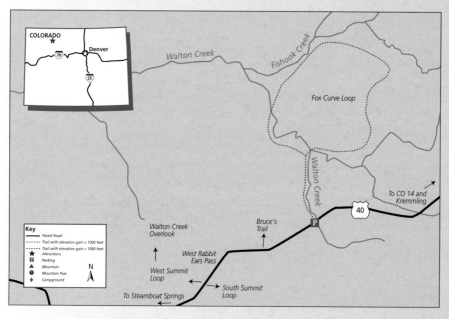

56. Hogan Park Trail

TOUR DISTANCE	2.3 miles each way
TOUR TIME	Out in 67 minutes, back in 83 minutes
STARTING ELEVATION	9,440 feet
HIGHEST ELEVATION	9,730 feet
ELEVATION GAIN	1,180 feet (includes 445 extra feet each way
DIFFICULTY	More difficult
AVALANCHE DANGER	Least
RELEVANT MAPS	Trails Illustrated Number 118 Mount Werner 7.5 minute Routt County Number Four Routt National Forest Routt National Forest

GETTING THERE: The trailhead is located on Rabbit Ears Pass off of U.S. 40 either 3.8 miles from East Rabbit Ears Pass summit or 3.7 miles from West Rabbit Ears Pass summit. Park off the south side of the highway. The Hogan Pak Trailhead is on the north side of U.S. 40.

COMMENT: The Hogan Park Trail extends from U.S. 40 on Rabbit Ears Pass to Mount Werner in Steamboat Springs. The entire trail is long and arduous, but the segment described here can be navigated by most winter trekkers and takes you through many lovely, vast meadows en route to an overlook of Fishhook Creek and Mount Werner. The blue diamond markers are frequent and well placed. Some are on trees and others are on poles in the large meadows. Snowshoers are urged to travel parallel to the skier's tracks rather than in them.

THE TOUR: Begin to the north from the Hogan Park sign on the north side of the highway. The first few hundred yards rise steeply. Continue north and exit the highway. As you pass through one meadow after another, revel in the backcountry experience. The trail eventually bends to the northwest as you climb and descend the hills. A good turnaround point is at a high clearing as Mount Werner comes into view to the northwest. A steep descent to Fishhook Creek lies ahead. Savor the moment before the return, which will take longer than your outgoing route.

SIDEBAR: POWDER

There is something about this north central area in Colorado that generates some of the finest powder skiing just about anywhere. It's extraordinarily light, and as you blast through it the cold crisp air is filled with sparkles. Think we are overdoing it a bit? Come up to Rabbit Ears Pass on a powder day—you'll see.

Going north on Hogan Park Trail.

PHOTO BY DAVE MULLER

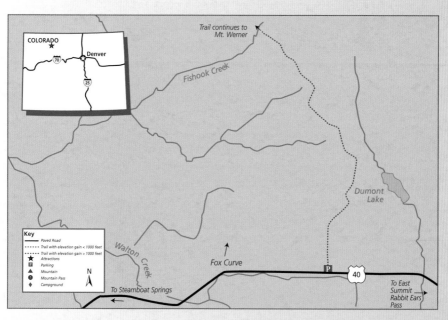

125

57. North Walton Peak Loop

TOUR DISTANCE	Up in 3.1 miles, down in 3.3 miles
TOUR TIME	Up in 96 minutes, down in 86 minutes.
STARTING ELEVATION	9,560 feet
HIGHEST ELEVATION	10,142 feet
ELEVATION GAIN	1,082 feet (includes 500 extra feet)
DIFFICULTY	More difficult
AVALANCHE DANGER	Moderate
RELEVANT MAPS	Trails Illustrated Number 118 Mount Werner 7.5 minute Walton Peak 7.5 minute Routt County Number Four

GETTING THERE: Take U.S. 40 northwest of Kremmling to the intersection with Colorado 14. Continue northwest on U.S. 40 from this intersection for 7 miles and park in the middle parking area on the left (south) side of the road.

COMMENT: This tour to North Walton Peak is intermediate in difficulty and reaches a high point with wonderful vistas. Don't confuse this tour with the one to Walton Peak, 1 mile to the south. Both are delightful outings.

THE TOUR: Begin south from the parking area and descend steeply on Trail 3A to Walton Creek. The Walton Creek Loop Trail then goes east and west. You go east and ascend by trail into the trees. (This is the easier leg of the loop.) Blue diamonds on the trees or blue ribbons mark these trails. You reach a fork and sign after 0.6 mile from the trailhead. You ascend left (south) on Trail 3C, and 0.4 mile farther you reach a road used by snowmobiles. Go to the right (south) and continue in a clockwise direction and upward into some beautiful open areas around a ridge. After 0.6 mile from the last fork, take the right fork and ascend to the west through an open area, and again proceed in a clockwise direction to the top of North Walton Peak. Two small huts with radio towers lie to your right near the summit. Take in the great view with Rabbit Ears Peak to the north northeast and Walton Peak nearby to the south southwest. Return as you ascended and take advantage of the many free skiing and snowshoeing opportunities. At the junction of Trail 3C and 3A, which you encountered after 0.6 mile on the ascent, go left (southwest) to complete the loop. Ascend steeply to a ridge and then go down to the southwest and west over a very steep section to return to the valley near Walton Creek. Go right at two successive forks past a green utility building and cross Walton Creek before ascending north to the parking area.

Carving turns on North Walton Peak ski hill.

PHOTO BY DAVE COOPER

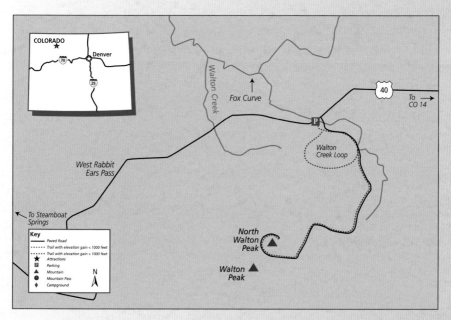

58. Par-a-lel Route

TOUR DISTANCE	2.5 miles each way
TOUR TIME	Out in 85 minutes, back in 75 minutes
STARTING ELEVATION	9,440 feet
HIGHEST ELEVATION	9,520 feet
ELEVATION GAIN	950 feet (includes 435 extra feet each way)
DIFFICULTY	More difficult
AVALANCHE DANGER	Least
RELEVANT MAPS	Trails Illustrated Number 118
	Mount Werner 7.5 minute
	Walton Peak 7.5 minute
	Routt County Number Four

GETTING THERE: On U.S. 40, drive to Rabbit Ears Pass southeast of Steamboat Springs. From East Rabbit Ears Pass, drive west 3.8 miles, or from West Rabbit Ears Pass drive east 3.7 miles. Park in the large area on the south side of the highway by the Walton Peak-Hogan Park Trailhead signs.

COMMENT: Rabbit Ears Pass offers a bonanza for winter outdoor recreationists. Nordic skiers and snowshoers generally use the central and western areas of the pass, while snowmobilers use the eastern segment. The Par-a-lel Route connects the Walton Creek Loop on the east with the South Summit Loop on the west.

THE TOUR: Begin by descending to the south southwest from the trailhead signs. Within 200 yards, take a right fork, cross an open area, and pass by the facilities of the Walton Creek Campground. Then take a right fork and ascend to the southwest. Blue diamond signs on the trees designate your way. Soon the trail curves to the right and ascends more steeply. Continue up and down along the trail, making sure to follow the blue diamonds. After 1.5 miles, descend into a vast meadow. Proceed along the meadow floor in a westerly direction, cross another vast clearing, and then gently ascend southwest. At yet another clearing, continue across, and then ascend to meet the South Summit Loop Trail coming from the west. This is your turnaround point unless you want to extend your outing by completing the 3.2 mile South Summit Loop, preferably in a counterclockwise direction.

SIDEBAR: POST-HOLING

Post-holing is the fine art of taking a step and sinking up to your knee, attempting another step with the same results, followed by another step and so on. It is a great way to get nowhere slowly and is often associated with leaving the trail to answer the call of nature. Good luck.

The western edge of Par-a-lel Route.

PHOTO BY DAVE MULLER

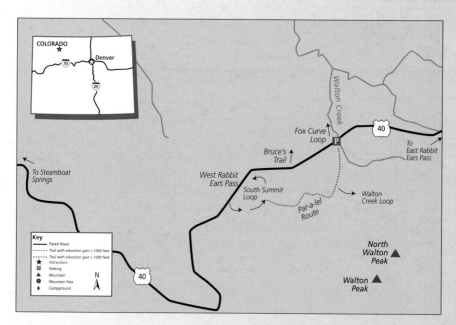

59. South Summit Loop

TOUR DISTANCE	3.2 miles (total loop)
TOUR TIME	76 minutes
STARTING ELEVATION	9,320 feet
HIGHEST ELEVATION	9,540 feet
ELEVATION GAIN	440 feet (includes 220 extra feet)
DIFFICULTY	More difficult
AVALANCHE DANGER	Least
RELEVANT MAPS	Trails Illustrated Number 118
	Mount Werner 7.5 minute
	Routt County Number Four
	Routt National Forest

GETTING THERE: Take U.S. 40 to the western edge of Rabbit Ears Pass (between Steamboat Springs to the northwest and Kremmling to the southeast). This area is 9.1 miles west of the junction of Colorado 14 and U.S. 40, or 13.9 miles southeast of 3rd Street and Lincoln Avenue (U.S. 40) in the town of Steamboat Springs. Park off the south side of the highway.

COMMENT: Rabbit Ears Pass is a paradise for winter recreation. One of the several circuit trails on the west side of the pass is the South Summit Loop, which is not used by snowmobilers. Trailhead signs provide diagrams and the distances of the various trails. Nordic skiers and snowshoers on Rabbit Ears Pass are urged to use trails marked by blue blazes. Snowmobilers are asked to follow the trails with orange blazes. The snowmobile trails are mostly on the eastern side of the flat pass.

THE TOUR: The South Summit Loop begins up into the forest to the southeast from the trailhead signboard. After 50 yards, there is a fork. This is the terminus of the South Summit Loop. The popular route is the counterclockwise one. Therefore, continue straight and steeply ahead. At 0.5 mile from the trailhead, you reach the high point of the loop near a small aspen grove. Now follow the blue blazes and blue ribbons down a steep run to the valley floor until you soon reach a huge, flat, open meadow. Continue along the left side of this clearing and pass the Meadows Campground on your left before curving left, back to your starting point. U.S. 40 will now be visible. Continue westerly parallel to a series of power poles until they eventually cross the highway to the northwest. Slowly ascend the well-marked trail along the northern edge of the forest, and finally reach the end of the loop in a small clearing. Then descend rapidly to the right and and to the trailhead, adjacent to the highway parking area.

A well-tracked trail on South Summit Loop.

PHOTO BY DAVE MULLER

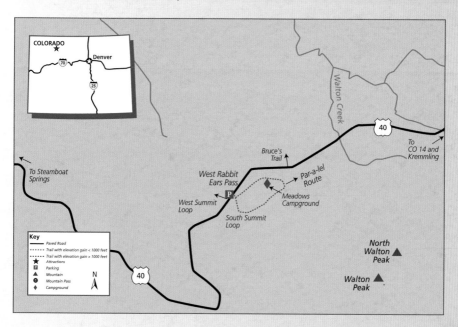

131

60. West Summit Loop 1A

TOUR DISTANCE	3.6 miles (total loop)
TOUR TIME	Up in 29 minutes, down in 47 minutes (counterclockwise loop)
STARTING ELEVATION	9,320 feet
HIGHEST ELEVATION	9,680 feet
ELEVATION GAIN	720 feet (includes 360 extra feet)
DIFFICULTY	More difficult
AVALANCHE DANGER	Least
RELEVANT MAPS	Trails Illustrated Number 118 Mount Werner 7.5 minute Steamboat Springs 7.5 minute Routt County Number Four Routt National Forest

GETTING THERE: On U.S. 40, drive to the western edge of Rabbit Ears Pass. This area is 9.1 miles west of the junction of Colorado 14 and U.S. 40, or 13.9 miles southeast of 3rd Street and Lincoln Avenue (U.S. 40) in Steamboat Springs.

COMMENT: Rabbit Ears Pass, a 7.6 mile mesa along U.S. 40, is the Garden of Eden for cross-country skiers and snowshoers in Colorado. (Be sure to bring an apple.) This outing begins from the west side of the pass and loops north through beautiful terrain and inviting open bowls to a high point with great views of Rabbit Ears Peak to the northeast. Walton Peak is to the southeast, and the Yampa Valley is to the southwest. The counterclockwise route continues to meander down through alternating forest and open meadows with many steep ups and downs.

THE TOUR: Begin north if you wish to travel the loop counterclockwise from the trailhead sign. (A trail ascends northwest if you want to travel in the opposite direction.) After 75 yards, keep right and follow the blue diamond tree blazes as the trail descends to a small crossing of the valley floor with highway traffic nearby on your right. This is the low point of this tour as the trail curves left (northwest) and then ascends a large, open basin to the west. Keep to the right of a series of power poles as the trail rises to a high point past several small aspen groves adjoining the evergreen forest. At the open high point, enjoy the inspiring panorama before continuing down to the southwest, and reenter the trees as the trail curves back and forth. Be sure to follow the blue diamond tree markers and occasional blue poles. After passing above a great bowl for free skiing, descend the ravine and then ascend a steep 100-yard slope with very few trees. The trail then falls and rises back to the trailhead and the completion of the West Summit Loop.

Wide open meadow on West Summit Loop 1A.

PHOTO BY DAVE MULLER

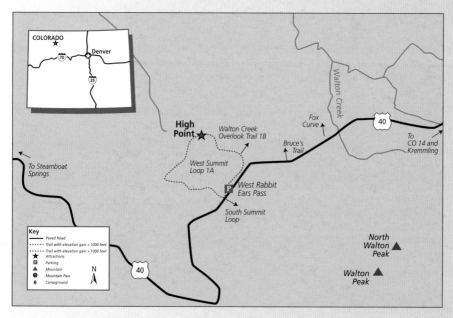

61. West Summit Loop 1B

TOUR DISTANCE	5.1 miles (total loop)
TOUR TIME	152 minutes
STARTING ELEVATION	9,320 feet
HIGHEST ELEVATION	9,520 feet
ELEVATION GAIN	625 feet (includes 425 extra feet)
DIFFICULTY	More difficult
AVALANCHE DANGER	Least
RELEVANT MAPS	Trails Illustrated Number 118 Mount Werner 7.5 minute Walton Peak 7.5 minute Routt County Number Four Routt National Forest

GETTING THERE: Drive to the West Summit of Rabbit Ears Pass on U.S. 40 and park off the north side of the highway near the trailhead signs. This trailhead is 7.5 miles west of the East Summit of Rabbit Ears Pass.

COMMENT: The Rabbit Ears Pass area is filled with wonderful cross-country ski and snowshoe trails. The vast, rolling terrain, many trails, and abundant snow make this a premier winter playground. This tour is the more easterly of two loops that begin to the north at the West Summit of the pass. Designated Loop 1B, this loop is also called the Walton Creek Overlook Loop. A counterclockwise direction will be described. Many prefer the clockwise direction. The trailhead sign understates the distance of this meandering loop, which is defined by the frequent blue trail markers.

THE TOUR: From the parking area and trailhead signboard, begin up to the north northwest. Keep straight for the first 100 yards, as Loop 1A leads to the left at a sign. Descend to the right following the blue trail blazes, and proceed parallel to U.S. 40 on your right. Emerge into a vast clearing, an intersection, and a sign. For this counterclockwise route on Loop 1B, continue to the right (east northeast). (You will return to this point at the end of the loop.) Cross the meadow, enter the trees, and gradually curve to the left as you ascend and descend through forest and clearings. Be sure to have blue markers always in sight. Around 3.5 miles, cross Walton Creek and ascend to a high point of this loop and a trail intersection. Descend the vast clearing to the left, and put your downhill technique to the test. Keep right at the junction with your Loop 1B starting point. Rise through the trees back to the trailhead on your original outbound route and pass Loop 1A on your right shortly before the trailhead.

The author on West Summit Loop 1B.

PHOTO BY JACKIE MULLER

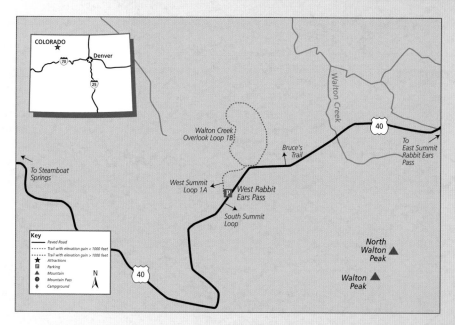

62. Alberta Falls

Tour Distance	0.9 mile each way
Tour Time	Up in 26 minutes, down in 22 minutes (snowshoer's times)
Starting Elevation	9,200
Highest Elevation	9,400
Elevation Gain	272 feet (includes 36 extra feet each way)
Difficulty	Easiest
Avalanche Danger	Least
Relevant Maps	Trails Illustrated Number 200
	Longs Peak 7.5 minute
	McHenry's Peak 7.5 minute
	Larimer County Number Three

GETTING THERE: From the Beaver Meadows Entrance to Rocky Mountain National Park (west of Estes Park on Highway 36), drive 0.2 mile into the park. Turn left and follow the Bear Lake Road for 8 miles. Park on the left at the Glacier Gorge Trailhead. A fee is required to enter Rocky Mountain National Park.

COMMENT: The wonderful web of trails near Bear Lake in Rocky Mountain National Park offers many possibilities for both winter and summer trekking. In summer, Alberta Falls features the roaring waters of Glacier Creek. In the winter, snow and ice cover the flow that proceeds out of view. Above the falls, you can continue to Mills Lake, Loch Vale, or Lake Haiyaha. Below, the falls and Glacier Creek flow into Sprague Lake and beyond to the Big Thompson River.

THE TOUR: Start out to the south southwest from the trailhead signboard. After 0.3 mile, pass a trail on the left that leads to Sprague Lake. Ascend 35 yards more to a T-intersection with signs. Continue to the left toward Loch Vale. Keep left at the fork and cross a bridge. Follow the main trail up to a sign at Alberta Falls as the route ascends to the right. There are delights beyond this point that may attract you. Note the winter beauty of the hibernating falls with Half Mountain towering beyond and above. Return as you ascended.

SIDEBAR: HEADLAMPS

We used to carry a small flashlight that we held in our teeth as we tried to accomplish a wide variety of things in the dark. We were always drooling on the flashlight and thinking that our dentist might put this activity right up there with chomping ice. Then we bought an LED headlamp, and everything became clear to us.

Alberta Falls with Half Mountain in the background.   PHOTO BY DAVE MULLER

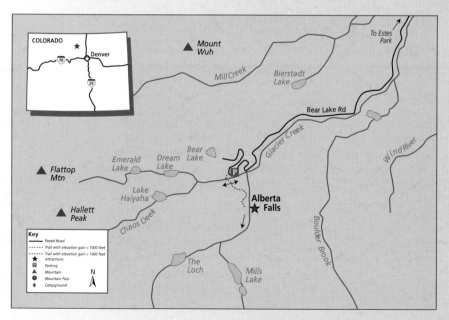

63. Bear Lake to Bierstadt Lake

TOUR DISTANCE	2.1 miles each way
TOUR TIME	Out in 50 minutes, back in 48 minutes
STARTING ELEVATION	9,475 feet
HIGHEST ELEVATION	9,720 feet
ELEVATION GAIN	710 feet (includes 465 extra feet)
DIFFICULTY	More difficult
AVALANCHE DANGER	Least
RELEVANT MAPS	Trails Illustrated Number 200 McHenrys Peak 7.5 minute Larimer County Number Three

GETTING THERE: From the Beaver Meadows Entrance in Rocky Mountain National Park, west of Estes Park on Highway 36, drive west 0.2 mile and turn left onto the paved Bear Lake Road. Drive for 9.2 miles and park in the large parking area at the road's end near Bear Lake. A fee is required to enter Rocky Mountain National Park.

COMMENT: Cross-country skiing can be daunting in Rocky Mountain National Park. Narrow, winding trails, limited snowfall, and the lack of old mining roads call for snowshoes as the preferable winter transport mode within the park. Touring skins are advised for the skier.

THE TOUR: Your trek begins on the trail leading southwest from the end of the Bear Lake parking area. Within 20 yards, turn right and follow the trail around the right side of Bear Lake to a signed fork. Ascend the steep right fork leading to Bierstadt Lake. Orange, square blazes on the trees mark the trail all the way to your destination as well as connecting trails. At 0.4 mile, go northeast up the right fork. The decreased winter foliage allows good views of the Glacier Gorge area on your right. After another 0.1 mile through healthy forest, you reach the high point of this outing with a great visual panorama of high peaks. Continue to your left (west) and descend quickly at a sharp curve of the trail to the right. At 1.1 miles of the tour, take the right (east) fork at another sign. Another 0.6 mile through thick forest brings you to another signed fork in a small clearing. Go left for another 0.1 mile and then right at another sign. Descend gradually 0.2 mile to a final fork and sign. Avoid the trail on the left, which continues around the lake. Take the right (south) fork around a log barrier for the final 50 yards to Bierstadt Lake. From here you can see Mount Lady Washington and Longs Peak to the south southwest over to Hallett Peak and Flattop Mountain to the west. Using your compass, carefully retrace your route back to Bear Lake.

A family outing on trail to Bierstadt Lake.

PHOTO COURTESY OF ROCKY MOUNTAIN NATIONAL PARK

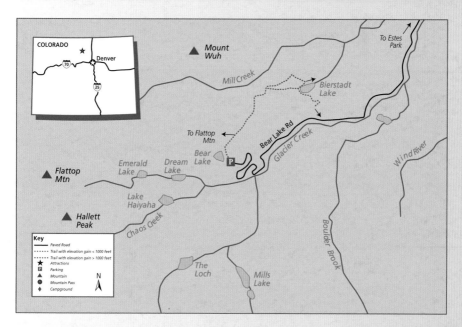

64. Bierstadt Lake

TOUR DISTANCE	1.2 miles each way
TOUR TIME	Up in 40 minutes, down in 35 minutes (snowshoer's time)
STARTING ELEVATION	8,870 feet
HIGHEST ELEVATION	9,430 feet
ELEVATION GAIN	620 feet (includes 30 extra feet each way)
DIFFICULTY	More difficult
AVALANCHE DANGER	Least
RELEVANT MAPS	Trails Illustrated Number 200 Longs Peak 7.5 minute Larimer County Number Three

GETTING THERE: Enter Rocky Mountain National Park at the Beaver Meadows Entrance station, west of Estes Park. Drive 0.2 mile to a junction. Turn left on the Bear Lake Road. After 6.5 miles on this road, park on the right where the Bierstadt Lake Trail begins. A fee is required to enter Rocky Mountain National Park.

COMMENT: This lake in Rocky Mountain National Park commemorates the work of German artist Albert Bierstadt, whose paintings include many scenes of the American West. This short trail switchbacks up to scenic Bierstadt Lake and is one of several ways to reach the lake. In winter, be careful to stay on the trail because deep snow can often obscure it. If you're lucky, you will encounter some wildlife, which roam freely and without fear in Rocky Mountain National Park. Snowshoers will likely enjoy this trail more than nordic skiers due to the steep, narrow switchbacks.

THE TOUR: Begin on the Bierstadt Lake Trail to the west northwest. As you follow the switchbacks up to the ridge, enjoy the great views across the valley to the south and southeast. The trail then descends from the ridge to a signed fork. The left hand trail leads to Bear Lake. Take the trail on the right and quickly reach Bierstadt Lake. A trail circles the lake.

SIDEBAR: ROCKY MOUNTAIN NATIONAL PARK

Through the efforts of F.O. Stanley, the inventor of the Stanley Steamer and builder of the Stanley Hotel, and naturalist Enos Mills, President Woodrow Wilson signed documents to initiate the creation of the park in 1915. Stanley supported the Estes Park Protective and Improvement Association, which protected wildflowers and wildlife and built roads and trails. Mills lectured, wrote letters and articles, and lobbied Congress for the establishment of a new 1,000 square mile National Park that would stretch from the Wyoming border to Pikes Peak. Most civic leaders supported the idea, as did the Denver Chamber of Commerce and the Colorado Mountain Club.

Early winter on Bierstadt Lake.

PHOTO BY DAVID HITE

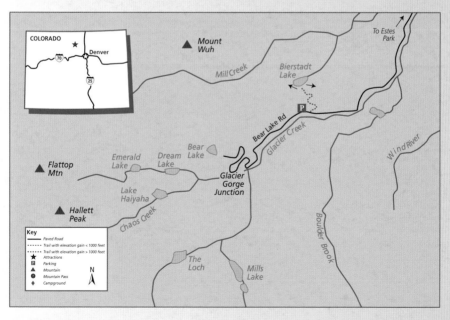

65. Calypso Cascades

TOUR DISTANCE	2.8 miles each way
TOUR TIME	Up in 80 minutes, down in 70 minutes (snowshoer's times)
STARTING ELEVATION	8,380 feet
HIGHEST ELEVATION	9,150 feet
ELEVATION GAIN	900 feet (includes 65 extra feet each way)
DIFFICULTY	More difficult
AVALANCHE DANGER	Least
RELEVANT MAPS	Trails Illustrated Number 200 Allens Park 7.5 minute Boulder County Roosevelt National Forest

GETTING THERE: From the junction with U.S. 36 at the west end of Lyons, drive southwest on Colorado 7 for 20.4 miles. Turn left into the Wild Basin Area. After 0.4 mile take the right fork, which leads past the Wild Basin Entrance to Rocky Mountain National Park. Follow the road into the park to a winter closure gate and park on the left. This is 1.5 miles from Colorado 7. A fee is required to enter Rocky Mountain National Park.

COMMENT: The Wild Basin Area in the southeast quadrant of Rocky Mountain National Park is a hub for summer hiking. In the winter, the crowds are smaller, but the area is no less beautiful. Trekking to the Calypso Cascades will be more enjoyable for the snowshoer, but a good nordic skier can enjoy it as well. Skiers should wait until January or when there is considerable snow depth.

THE TOUR: Start out on the road to the southwest around the road barrier. Quickly cross a bridge over North Saint Vrain Creek and follow the wide road past the Finch Lake Trailhead on the left. You arrive at another crossing on the North Saint Vrain Creek 1 mile from the trailhead. Go left at the fork and you will rapidly reach a Wild Basin Trails signboard. Continue over a side creek and proceed up the valley with North Saint Vrain Creek on your left. At 2.5 miles from the trailhead, cross the creek on a bridge and ascend more steeply the final 0.3 mile to a trail fork, signs, and bridges at the Calypso Cascades. In the summer, the rushing water here is impressive. In the winter, the snow and ice project a different beauty. Savor the moment before your return.

A happy skier on the trail to Calypso Cascades.

PHOTO COURTESY OF ROCKY MOUNTAIN NATIONAL PARK

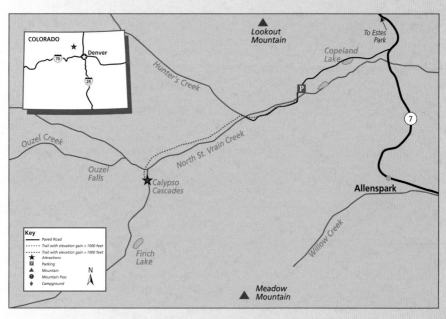

66. Emerald Lake

TOUR DISTANCE	1.8 miles each way
TOUR TIME	Up in 60 minutes, down in 48 minutes (snowshoer's time)
STARTING ELEVATION	9,475 feet
HIGHEST ELEVATION	10,140 feet
ELEVATION GAIN	850 feet (includes 185 extra feet)
DIFFICULTY	Easiest
AVALANCHE DANGER	Least
RELEVANT MAPS	Trails Illustrated Number 200 McHenry's Peak 7.5 minute Larimer County Number Three

GETTING THERE: From the Beaver Meadows Entrance in Rocky Mountain National Park, west of Estes Park on Highway 36, drive 0.2 mile and turn left onto Bear Lake Road. Follow this good, scenic road for 9.2 miles to the end of the road at the large Bear Lake parking area. A fee is required to enter Rocky Mountain National Park.

COMMENT: It can be argued that Rocky Mountain National Park is even more beautiful in the winter than the summer. Certainly there are smaller crowds. If the weather is good, this tour to Emerald Lake can be a real delight. Starting at Bear Lake, two other lakes, Nymph Lake and Dream Lake, are passed en route to Emerald Lake, situated in a rocky bowl with Hallett Peak towering above. The narrow trails and windblown snow conditions render most trails in Rocky Mountain National Park more suitable for snowshoers, but nordic skiers with good skills can enjoy the park as well. This tour is no exception.

THE TOUR: From the upper parking area, begin west southwest. At the signs take a quick left and then a right fork as this excellent trail ascends past small Nymph Lake after 0.5 mile. After another 0.6 mile and right fork (the left fork leads to Lake Haiyaha), you pass long, narrow Dream Lake before the final ascent to a high point and a short decent to Emerald Lake. Return as you ascended and enjoy the combination of blue sky, green pine trees, and pure white snow.

SIDEBAR: MAPS

We have added maps to this guidebook because we wanted to give you some sense of what the route is like. But they do not replace the detailed maps listed with each tour. In the data section of these route descriptions, we have listed some maps that have the route on them because it is essential that when you get lost (and we all do at one time or another), you have a reference for finding your way.

Emerald Lake Trailhead.

PHOTO BY DAVE MULLER

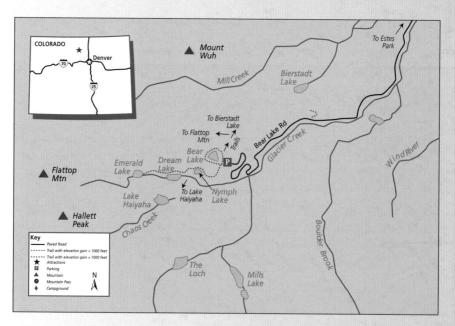

67. Glacier Creek Trail to Bear Lake

TOUR DISTANCE	3.3 miles each way
TOUR TIME	Up in 104 minutes, down in 74 minutes (snowshoer's time)
STARTING ELEVATION	8,670 feet
HIGHEST ELEVATION	9,475
ELEVATION GAIN	1,029 feet (including 112 extra feet each way)
DIFFICULTY	Most difficult
AVALANCHE DANGER	Least
RELEVANT MAPS	Trails Illustrated Number 200 Longs Peak 7.5 minute McHenry's Peak 7.5 minute Larimer County Number Three

GETTING THERE: From the Beaver Meadows Entrance in Rocky Mountain National Park, west of Estes Park on Highway 36, drive 0.2 mile into the park. Then turn left onto Bear Lake Road and drive for 5.7 more miles. Turn left toward the Sprague Lake parking area. Turn right after 0.1 mile, and park in the large lot after another 0.3 mile. A fee is required to enter Rocky Mountain National Park.

COMMENT: The Glacier Creek Trail, like all the trails in Rocky Mountain National Park, is well-marked with signs and orange metal tree markers. It continues up to Bear Lake. Wait for a fresh snowfall and a calm day to try this outing because snow depth and heavy winds can be a winter problem in the park.

THE TOUR: Start out by heading southeast to the Glacier Creek Trail signboard. From here, ascend gradually to the right (south southwest). Pass a trail on the left to Sprague Lake after 0.3 mile. Another 0.3 mile brings you to a five-way intersection with signs. Take the third trail from the left, which leads west southwest toward Bear Lake. Continue winding your way through the woods, with occasional glimpses of rocky Hallett Peak. The meandering trail parallels Glacier Creek, and you will see a sign 2.8 miles into the tour. From here, ascend to the left (west southwest) 40 yards to another trail junction with signs. Keep right, cross a bridge, pass a signboard, and follow the sign up to the left for the final 0.5 mile to Bear Lake. Just before the lake, the trail to Emerald, Dream, and Nymph Lakes is passed on the left. Enjoy popular and scenic Bear Lake, which lies just above a huge parking area on the right. Unless you have a second vehicle at the lake, retrace your route back to the Glacier Creek Trailhead near Sprague Lake.

TOP: Hallett Peak and Flattop Mountain from Glacier Creek Trail.
BOTTOM: Glacier Creek. PHOTOS COURTESY OF ROCKY MOUNTAIN NATIONAL PARK

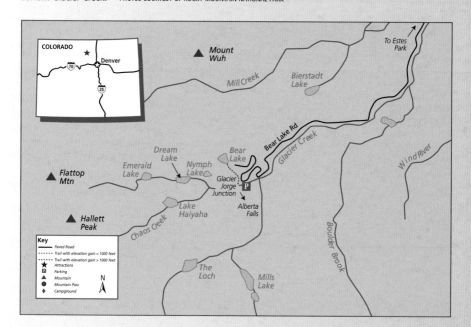

68. The Loch

TOUR DISTANCE	3 miles each way
TOUR TIME	Up in 92 minutes, down in 82 minutes (snowshoer's time)
STARTING ELEVATION	9,200 feet
HIGHEST ELEVATION	10,180 feet
ELEVATION GAIN	1,355 feet (includes 375 extra feet)
DIFFICULTY	More difficult (for the snowshoer), most difficult (for the nordic skier)
AVALANCHE DANGER	Least
RELEVANT MAPS	Trails Illustrated Number 200 or 301 McHenry's Peak 7.5 minute Larimer County Number Three

GETTING THERE: From the Beaver Meadows Entrance in Rocky Mountain National Park on the west side of Estes Park on Highway 36, drive 0.2 mile into the park, turn left onto the Bear Lake Road, and follow it for 8 miles. Park on the left at the Glacier Gorge parking area and the trailhead. A fee is required to enter Rocky Mountain National Park.

COMMENT: The trails in Rocky Mountain National Park are always clear and well marked with signs. This tour to the Loch (also called Loch Vale) will be relatively easy for the snowshoer but quite challenging for the nordic skier. A side trail off the main trail allows the skier to avoid some of the rocks and possible bare spots on the main trail.

THE TOUR: From the parking lot area begin to the south southwest from the trailhead signboard. Descend to a bridge creek crossing and pass a trail on the left of Sprague Lake. Ascend to a signed fork. The trail on the right leads to Bear Lake. Ascend to the left to a side trail on the right (south) just before reaching a third bridge crossing. This side trail is shorter and steeper and provides deeper snow; and it connects with the main trail in less than 1 mile. If you prefer the main trail, continue over the bridge and up to frozen Alberta Falls, which is marked by a sign. Follow the clear sign to the Loch as you rise to a five-way intersection. The trail to Mills Lake leads left, another trail to Lake Haiyaha goes right, and the side trail mentioned earlier joins the main trail from below on the right. Continue straight (west) to the Loch, which is 0.8 mile farther. You will at times leave the main trail and follow the tracks left by earlier trekkers. Finally the Loch will come into view as you cross over a ridge. The Sharktooth and Otis Peak loom over the lake. There are other destinations beyond the Loch for those seeking a greater challenge. Retrace your route on the return back to the trailhead.

Kent Krieder on a typical day at The Loch.

PHOTO BY DAVE MULLER

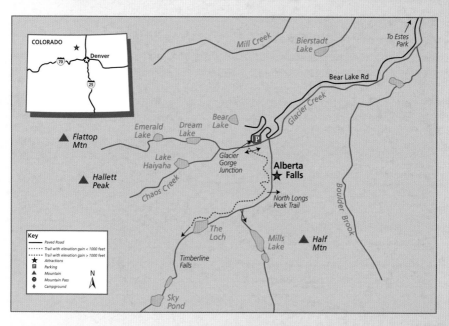

69. East Inlet Trail

TOUR DISTANCE	2 miles each way
TOUR TIME	Up in 51 minutes, down in 46 minutes
STARTING ELEVATION	8,391 feet
HIGHEST ELEVATION	8,640 feet
ELEVATION GAIN	609 feet (includes 180 extra feet each way)
DIFFICULTY	More difficult
AVALANCHE DANGER	Least
RELEVANT MAPS	Trails Illustrated Number 200 Shadow Mountain 7.5 minute Grand County Number Two

GETTING THERE: From the eastern edge of the town of Grand Lake, leave Grand Avenue and drive northeast up the West Portal Road for 1.9 miles. Keep left at the fork and park on the left at the East Inlet Trailhead after another 0.1 mile.

COMMENT: Winter touring in the western side of Rocky Mountain National Park can be very gratifying. There are fewer people on the trail, snowmobiles and pets are not allowed in the park, and the snow is usually ample. This tour follows the East Inlet Trail and ends at the far end of a second large meadow. En route, a side loop trail on the right leads to Adams Falls. The narrow winding trail has steep sections that are easier for the snowshoer than the cross-country skier.

THE TOUR: Begin up to the southeast with a wooden fence on each side of the trail. Then descend into the forest before rising steeply to the Adams Falls side trails. A first large meadow is reached shortly thereafter as you continue along its left side. The trail rises and falls with the East Inlet Creek always on your right before reaching the edge of a second large meadow. Mount Craig looms on the right before reaching the far end on the valley on your right. The trail steepens here and rises to several distant lakes.

SIDEBAR: FIRST AID KIT

We've assembled our own first aid kit that tends to reflect our proclivities for injury. We carry moleskin for blisters, various sizes of bandages (that we replace every year if we don't use them), and antibiotic salve for small cuts and burns. Prepacked sanitary wipes are a good idea for cleaning up a wound or a burn. We also carry a light little book called *First Aid: Pocket Guide,* 4th edition, published by the Mountaineers. It folds right into our first aid kit and is the first thing, along with a pair of latex gloves, to pop up when the kit is opened.

TOP: Lake Verna above the East Inlet Trail. PHOTO BY DAVID HITE

BOTTOM: East Inlet trailhead. PHOTO BY DAVE MULLER

To Rocky Mountain National Park

COLORADO

Denver

Pettingell Lake

Lake Nokoni

North Inlet

West Portal Road

Mount Enentah

Ptarmigan Mountain

Shadow Mtn. Lake

Grand Lake

East Inlet Trail

Mount Cairns

Lone Pine Lake

East Inlet

Meadow

Adams Falls

Shadow Mountain

Key

- —— Paved Road
- - - - - Trail with elevation gain < 1000 feet
- ······ Trail with elevation gain > 1000 feet
- ★ Attractions
- 🅿 Parking
- ▲ Mountain
- ⊙ Mountain Pass
- ◆ Campground

N

70. Milner Pass

TOUR DISTANCE	6.6 miles each way
TOUR TIME	Up in 140 minutes, down in 68 minutes
STARTING ELEVATION	9,095 feet
HIGHEST ELEVATION	10,758 feet
ELEVATION GAIN	1,675 feet (includes 6 extra feet each way)
DIFFICULTY	More difficult
AVALANCHE DANGER	Least
RELEVANT MAPS	Trails Illustrated Number Two Fall River pass 7.5 minute Grand County Number Two

GETTING THERE: From the Grand Lake Entrance in Rocky Mountain National Park, drive north on U.S. 34 for 9.5 miles until the road plowing ends. Park here near the Timber Lake Trailhead. A fee is required to enter Rocky Mountain National Park.

COMMENT: In the winter months Trail Ridge Road is blocked off. However, the road is wide and gradual and also makes for good ski touring and snowshoeing when the snow is adequate. This lengthy tour involves a series of horseshoe curves en route to the Continental Divide at Milner Pass.

THE TOUR: Start northwest from the parking area and then quickly turn right (north) and follow Trail Ridge Road as it winds upward in a series of horseshoe curves. To the west lie the peaks of the Never Summer Range. Midway up the road there are great views south down the valley toward the Grand Lake area. Eventually you'll reach Milner Pass, with frozen Poudre Lake just beyond. Enjoy some rest and refreshment here before your long and winding downhill return back to the parking area near the Timber Lake and Colorado River Trailheads.

SIDEBAR: PLAN B

If you look closely at why people get in trouble in the backcountry, it is usually not because of one stunningly bad piece of luck, but any number of smaller mistakes committed beforehand. So you get a late start. The car is acting strangely as you climb out of the flatlands and into the mountains. Once you get to the trailhead, you find that an important piece of gear is missing and you are developing a throbbing headache. Stop! It just isn't your day to go snowshoeing or cross-country skiing. It is your day for Plan B. Pack up your gear and go home. If you continue your outing, there is a good chance that things will just keep getting worse and that you will get into real trouble. By going home you end the string of mistakes. The trail and the mountains will be there for another day.

Western trailhead to Milner Pass.

PHOTO BY DAVE MULLER

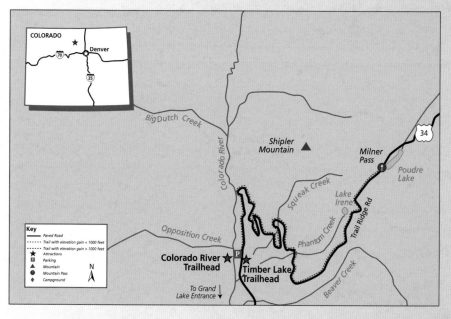

71. Shipler Cabin

TOUR DISTANCE	2.3 miles
TOUR TIME	Up in 64 minutes, down in 62 minutes
STARTING ELEVATION	9,060 feet
HIGHEST ELEVATION	9,250 feet
ELEVATION GAIN	760 feet (includes 285 extra feet each way)
DIFFICULTY	More difficult
AVALANCHE DANGER	Moderate at Shipler Park
RELEVANT MAPS	Trails Illustrated Number 200 Fall River Pass 7.5 minute Grand County Number Two

GETTING THERE: From the west entrance to Rocky Mountain National Park, north of Grand Lake, drive north for 9.4 miles and take the left fork just before the road block. After another 0.2 mile, park at the Colorado River Trailhead. A fee is required to enter Rocky Mountain National Park.

COMMENT: The ruins of a cabin built in 1876 by Joseph L. Shipler, a miner and Civil War veteran, is the destination of this winter trek. The good trail passes along the eastern side of the headwaters of the Colorado River and is called the Colorado River Trail. Park rules forbid pets, snowmobiles, and guns. The best time for this outing is mid-winter when there are good snow conditions.

THE TOUR: From the parking area, begin to the north from the trailhead signboard. Within 150 yards, there is a steep ascent before the trail becomes more level. With the Colorado River always on your left, a signed fork is reached after 0.5 mile. The left fork is the Red Mountain Trail, which ascends to the aqueduct known as the Grand Ditch. Continue straight up the valley. Orange metal tree markers help identify the trail. Around 1.8 miles, the trail leaves the trees and emerges into a large, flat meadow known as Shipler Park. The trail passes directly below Shipler Mountain with some potential avalanche chutes. You can veer left to the center of the meadow to be more secure. At the end of the meadow lies the Shipler Cabin ruin on the right. This is a good turnaround point because the trail, 1.4 miles further up the valley to the former site of Lulu City, eventually becomes very demanding.

SIDEBAR: DEHYDRATION

When you are cross-country skiing or snowshoeing you are losing more water through perspiration and respiration than you might suspect. They symptoms of dehydration are headache, dizziness, and, in more severe cases, fainting. Cramps can also occur. The rule of thumb is simply to drink often when you are exercising.

TOP: A view from the track to Shipler Cabin.
BOTTOM: Ruins of Shipler Cabin.

PHOTOS BY DAVE MULLER

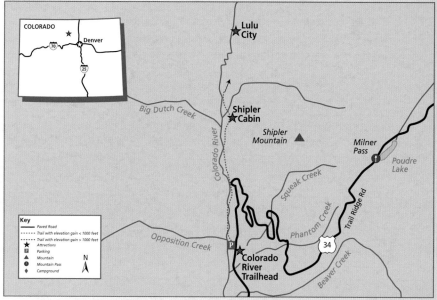

72. Sun Valley River Trail Loop

TOUR DISTANCE	2.5 miles (total loop)
TOUR TIME	66 minutes
STARTING ELEVATION	8,708 feet
HIGHEST ELEVATION	8,800 feet
ELEVATION GAIN	244 feet (includes 152 extra feet)
DIFFICULTY	More difficult
AVALANCHE DANGER	Least
RELEVANT MAPS	Trails Illustrated Number 200 Grand Lake 7.5 minute Grand County Number Two

GETTING THERE: From the entrance station to Rocky Mountain National Park, north of Grand Lake, drive north on U.S. 34 (Trail Ridge Road) for 0.7 mile. Park on the left at the Harbison Picnic Area. A fee is required to enter Rocky Mountain National Park.

COMMENT: The Sun Valley River Trail Loop, located on the southwestern edge of Rocky Mountain National Park, is a well-marked combination of the Valley Trail and the River Trail. The loop can be negotiated in either direction. A counterclockwise route will be described here. The trail is mostly level with a few steep sections and is marked with orange metal indicators on trees and periodic trail signs. The middle segment passes above the Colorado River. Dogs and vehicles are forbidden.

THE TOUR: Begin west and quickly reach a fork as you enter the forest. This is the beginning of the loop. Take the right fork and continue straight, parallel to U.S. 34. Follow the orange markers at the occasional intersections. At 0.7 mile from your starting point, go left (west) at the signed fork on the Valley Trail. Ascend gradually and navigate some steep descents as you cross the Powerline Trail and pass the Stock Trail on the left en route to the banks of the Colorado River. Turn left (south) on the River Trail at the end of the Valley Trail for another 0.7 mile and again pass the Stock Trail on the left. Continue to the south above the marshes and the river. Soon you will reach a T-intersection. Go left on the Valley Trail to complete the loop back to your starting point.

SIDEBAR: EXTRA CLOTHING

Bring an extra hat and a pair of gloves. Even though the probability is low that you will really need them, you'll be glad you packed them if they are needed—trust me.

Jackie Muller and Mamie Gardner on Sun Valley River Trail Loop.

PHOTO BY DAVE MULLER

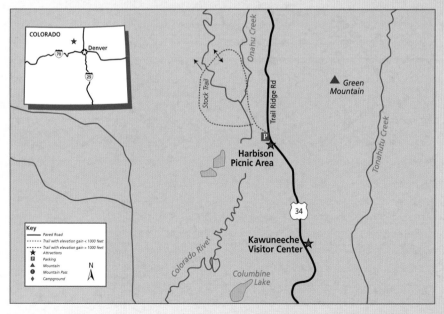

73. Tonahutu Trail to Kawuneeche Visitor Center

TOUR DISTANCE	1.5 miles each way
TOUR TIME	Up in 42 minutes, down in 36 minutes
STARTING ELEVATION	8,700 feet
HIGHEST ELEVATION	8,840 feet
ELEVATION GAIN	194 feet (includes 27 extra feet each way)
DIFFICULTY	Easiest
AVALANCHE DANGER	Least
RELEVANT MAPS	Trails Illustrated Number 200 Grand Lake 7.5 minute Grand County Number Two Rocky Mountain National Park

GETTING THERE: From Grand Avenue on the eastern side of the town of Grand Lake, drive northeast up the West Portal Road for 0.7 mile. Turn left up a steep road for another 0.3 mile and park at the Tonahutu Trailhead. If all the parking spaces are full, park back down the road.

COMMENT: The Tonahutu Trail leads to Big Meadows and beyond, deep into Rocky Mountain National Park. This short tour rises to a four-way intersection and the Tonahutu Spur Trail on the left. This spur trail then leads to the Kawuneeche Visitor Center, which makes a good destination and turnaround point.

THE TOUR: Begin on foot up to the west from the trailhead signboard. Quickly reach a steep upward grade before the trail becomes more gradual. Tonahutu Creek is always on your right. Pass a side trail to the Grand Lake Lodge and continue up the valley to a four-way intersection. Going straight leads to Big Meadows, but you proceed to the left and wind your way through lodgepole pine on the Tonahutu Spur Trail. This trail ends at the western visitor center for Rocky Mountain National Park. Discover the many features of this center before the return to your starting point.

SIDEBAR: LAYERING

We are great fans of wool, polypro, and fleece, particularly the latter two because they are lightweight, quick drying, and don't give off that wooly smell when wet. We also recommend layering so that you can add or take off clothing as the conditions and exertion dictate. Here is a typical example of layering: Begin with polypro long johns and thin polypro socks. Follow this with a light fleece shirt and synthetic water-resistant pants and then a middle-weight fleece pullover and waterproof wind pants. Add another layer of thick polypro or wool socks. Finish with a waterproof and breathable jacket, gloves or mittens, and boots and gaiters.

Tony Bianchi at Tonahutu Trailhead.

PHOTO BY DAVE MULLER

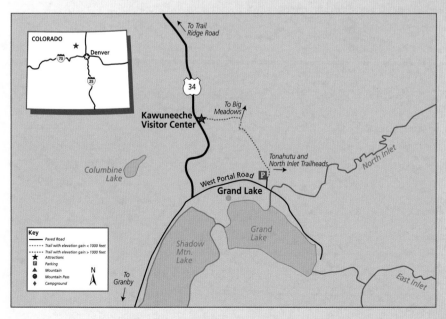

74. Baker's Tank

TOUR DISTANCE	3.3 miles each way
TOUR TIME	Up in 95 minutes, down in 60 minutes
STARTING ELEVATION	10,350 feet
HIGHEST ELEVATION	11,050 feet
ELEVATION GAIN	1,140 feet (includes 470 extra feet)
DIFFICULTY	Most difficult
AVALANCHE DANGER	Least
RELEVANT MAPS	Trails Illustrated Number 109
	Breckenridge 7.5 minute
	Boreas Pass 7.5 minute
	Summit County Number Two
	Arapaho National Forest – Dillon Ranger District

GETTING THERE: From the intersection and traffic light at Ski Hill Road in Breckenridge, drive south on Colorado 9 for 0.6 mile and turn left onto the Boreas Pass Road. Drive 3.8 miles to a parking area at the Baker's Tank trailhead. En route to this parking area from Colorado 9, keep right after 200 feet and again at 0.7 mile. Then go left at 1.2 miles and right at both 2 miles and 3.4 miles.

COMMENTS: A new forest trail has been created for nordic skiers and snowshoers east of the Boreas Pass Road to the Baker's Tank. The traditional route has been on the gradual, wide road, which was formerly a railroad bed. It is still available but more crowded. This new trail is much more demanding as it rises and falls through the woods. On the western slopes of Bald Mountain, the snow will often be better than on the road. The heavy foot and pet traffic on the Boreas Pass Road will also be avoided.

THE TOUR: Begin to the south southwest from the parking area at Baker's Tank Trail sign on the left. Enter the forest and follow the blue diamond blazes on the trees. These mark the narrow winding trail as it ascends rather steeply at times before descending to a drainage area around the halfway point. (The Boreas Pass Road is readily accessible from here to the right.) Continue by trail as it rises to the high point of this outing and a junction. A trail leads sharply to the left, but you turn right and continue to parallel the road as the trail now gradually descends to a meadow just above Baker's Tank on the right. This tank was used to supply water to locomotives that ran between Como and Breckenridge. On your ascent route to Baker's Tank there are only occasional views of the high peaks in this area. When you arrive at the Tank, you are rewarded with a lovely panorama.

Part of the panorama from Baker's Tank.

PHOTO BY DAVE MULLER

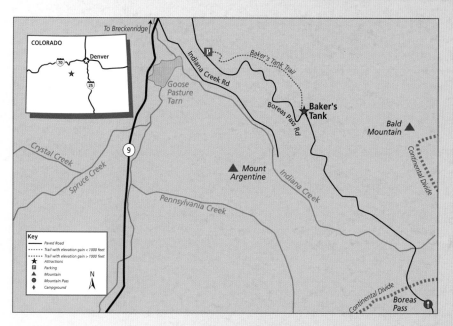

161

75. Bemrose Ski Circus to Hoosier Pass

TOUR DISTANCE	4.5 miles each way
TOUR TIME	Up in 105 minutes, down in 90 minutes
STARTING ELEVATION	10,590 feet
HIGHEST ELEVATION	11,570 feet
ELEVATION GAIN	1,730 feet (includes 375 extra feet each way)
DIFFICULTY	More difficult
AVALANCHE DANGER	Moderate at higher elevations
RELEVANT MAPS	Trails Illustrated Number 109 Breckenridge 7.5 minute Alma 7.5 minute Summit County Number Two Arapaho National Forest – Dillon Ranger District

GETTING THERE: From the traffic light at South Park Avenue in Breckenridge, drive south on Colorado 9 for 8.3 miles and turn left onto County Road 670. The cutoff is 1.6 miles north of Hoosier Pass. Park after 0.1 mile near the Bemrose Creek Ski Circus sign and map on the right.

COMMENT: At the southern end of Summit County near Hoosier Pass is a fine network of cross-country ski and snowshoe routes known as the Bemrose Creek Ski Circus. This route begins near Bemrose Creek and ascends on the steep Woods Trail to meet the Flume Trail, which then leads west to Hoosier Pass on level terrain. Hoosier Pass lies on the Continental Divide. Beautiful high peaks surround the area.

THE TOUR: Check the map on the trailhead sign and begin southeast either on the road or off the right side of the road. Continue generally east and, after 0.3 mile, ascend past a cabin on the left. Enter the Woods Trail through the trees. There are occasional blue diamond markers on the trees to indicate your route. Rise steeply up the valley with Bemrose Creek on the left. You will reach a clearing after 1.3 miles from the trailhead. Follow the tracks upward to join the Flume Trail at Junction Gulch. A sign on a tree near the junction is not easy to see. Take the right fork and continue southwest in an old aqueduct. There are some gentle ups and downs and occasional skiing or snowshoeing along some easy ledges. After 1 mile on the Flume Trail there is a fork. Take either route because they connect within 50 yards. As you pass various drainage areas, side trails may ascend to your left. At Hoosier Pass there is another Bemrose Creek Ski Circus sign. This is the turn-around point. Mount Lincoln, a "Fourteener", and North Star Mountain lie to the west. Return by your ascent route and take the left fork at Junction Gulch. The steep descent on the narrow Woods Trail requires care and skill.

Ginni Greer with North Star Mountain to the left and Quandary Peak to the right.

PHOTO BY DAVE COOPER

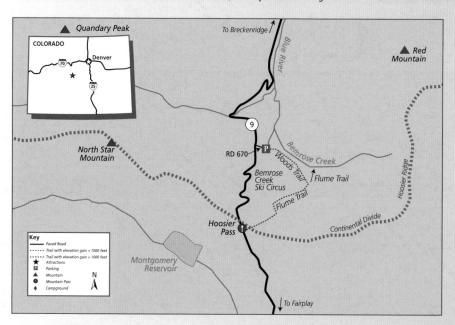

163

76. Burro Trail

TOUR DISTANCE	3.1 miles each way
TOUR TIME	Up in 80 minutes, down in 40 minutes
STARTING ELEVATION	9,960 feet
HIGHEST ELEVATION	10,610 feet
ELEVATION GAIN	900 feet (includes 250 extra feet)
DIFFICULTY	More difficult
AVALANCHE DANGER	Least
RELEVANT MAPS	Trails Illustrated Number 109 Breckenridge 7.5 minute Summit County Number two Arapaho National Forest— Dillon Ranger District

GETTING THERE: Park in the large free area between Main Street and Park Avenue in central Breckenridge, then take the free shuttle bus to the Beaver Run ski area (red route). The trailhead is marked by a sign at the edge of the forest at the southeast part of the Beaver Run area.

COMMENT: Mixing with downhill skiers, sheltering from the wind, and avoiding snowmobiles are features of the Burro Trail in Breckenridge. The route ascends through the forest before leveling off for the last 1.5 mile. Ideal for snowshoers, the downhill runs require intermediate skills for the cross-country skier.

THE TOUR: From the shuttle bus, proceed south across the Beaver Run area to the trailhead sign. Then begin southeast into the trees and across a creek. Quickly arrive at a fork. Keep right and avoid the steep ascending trail on the left. Follow the blue diamond markers on the trees and continue upward to join a level road around the halfway mark of this outing. Go to the left as the trail becomes more level and arrives at a crossing of the Crystal Creek Road, which ascends to the right. Continue straight across the road another 0.1 mile and descend gradually to reach the wide Spruce Creek Road and the turnaround point. The return will challenge the skier in the lower half of the trail.

SIDEBAR: DAY PACK

Don't go on a day trip with a 5,000 cubic inch expedition pack. It's too much gear and your companions will make fun of you. Instead, take a well-made and fitted day pack with 1,500 to 2,000 cubic inches of packing space. That should be more than enough for the Ten Essentials, including a water bottle, your lunch, some back-up gloves and a hat, some extra clothing, and something to sit on. There will even be plenty of room left over for a camera or whatever else you want to pack along.

TOP: Near the Burro trailhead.   PHOTO BY DAVE MULLER
BOTTOM: Burro Trail sign.   PHOTO BY DAVID HITE

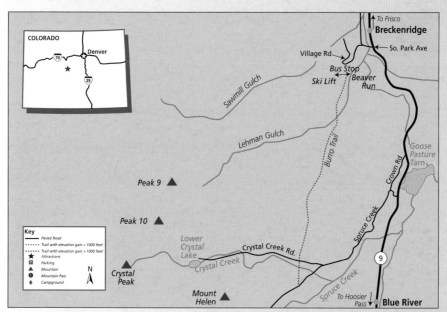

77. Corral Creek

TOUR DISTANCE	1.7 miles from trailhead to high point, 2.3 miles from high point to southern terminus, and 1.6 miles from southern terminus back to trailhead for a total of 5.6 miles.
TOUR TIME	49 minutes to high point, 46 minutes to southern terminus, and 60 minutes back to trailhead
STARTING ELEVATION	10,610 feet
HIGHEST ELEVATION	11,120 feet
ELEVATION GAIN	1,055 feet (includes 545 extra feet)
DIFFICULTY	More difficult
AVALANCHE DANGER	Least
RELEVANT MAPS	Trails Illustrated Number 108 Vail Pass 7.5 minute Summit County Number Two Eagle County Number Four

GETTING THERE: On Interstate 70 between Vail and Copper Mountain, drive to exit 190. Park in the designated area off the west side of the bridge that crosses the highway.

COMMENT: Winter use of the Corral Creek Basin, east of Vail Pass, involves a fee and a designated parking area. These requirements are part of the Vail Pass Recreation Area program to improve and control outdoor use in this popular area. While the Shrine Pass area, west of Vail Pass, is more heavily used, Corral Creek is free of snowmobiles and great for freestyle cross-country skiing and snowshoeing.

THE TOUR: From your parked vehicle, walk east on the bridge over Interstate 70. Begin on skis or snowshoes to the east. Within 10 feet of the road, turn left (north) and follow a series of blue diamond tree blazes into the forest. Continue steeply upward to reach a ridge with few trees 0.5 mile from the trailhead. You are now overlooking the Corral Creek Basin and have many choices of route. The standard route runs from north to south for 2.3 miles. You connect with this trail running north and south around its middle. You can ascend to the north to end at a treeless, snow-covered mound with great views back to the south. (The prominent mountain to the north is Uneva Peak; in the distance to the south is Jacque Peak). Alternatively, descend southward 1.1 miles to reach the southern limit of the trail at Interstate 70, just north of the bridge over Corral Creek. Many open areas invite exploration. If no clear route is discernible, proceed parallel to and west of Corral Creek. For your return, proceed back to the initial ridge that gave you the first view into the Corral Creek Basin. The final 0.5 mile back to the trailhead and bridge over Interstate 70 is quite steep.

A view from Corral Creek near I-70.

PHOTO BY DAVE MULLER

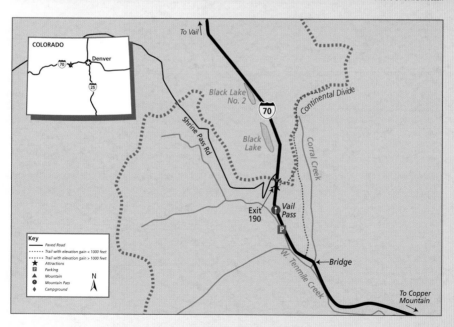

167

78. Flume Trail

TOUR DISTANCE	2.5 miles each way
TOUR TIME	Out in 58 minutes, back in 52 minutes
STARTING ELEVATION	11,539 feet
HIGHEST ELEVATION	11,550 feet
ELEVATION GAIN	961 feet (includes 475 extra feet each way)
DIFFICULTY	Easiest
AVALANCHE DANGER	Moderate
RELEVANT MAPS	Trails Illustrated Number 109
	Alma 7.5 minute
	Summit County Number Two
	Arapaho National Forest— Dillon Ranger District

GETTING THERE: Take Colorado 9 to Hoosier Pass, located between Breckenridge to the north and Fairplay to the south. Park at the pass in the open area on the west side of the road.

COMMENT: The Flume Trail begins at Hoosier Pass on the Continental Divide. From here you can see great distances into South Park, as well as the Tenmile Range and the Dillon Valley to the north. Because of its high elevation, the snow is usually good until early April. The route follows an old aqueduct that rises and falls gently along the northern flanks of the Hoosier Ridge. At its northeastern terminus, the Flume Trail connects with the Woods Trail and the Bemrose Creek Trail. Both of these are part of the so-called Bemrose Ski Circus and lead west to a parking area off of Colorado 9 that is 1.6 miles north of Hoosier Pass.

THE TOUR: Walk carefully east over the highway from the Hoosier Pass parking area to a sign and map. Begin your trek to the north and enter the trees on the narrow channel known as the Flume. Follow the mostly level trail northeast and cross the first of three major drainages in an open area. During your 2.5-mile outward journey along the Flume, you mostly follow a tree-lined path with good views, especially to the north and northwest. Occasional side routes offer themselves for exploration. Blue diamond blazes mark the trail. Around the halfway point, you briefly traverse a fairly steep side slope. A good turnaround point comes at a signed fork at Junction Gulch. The left fork descends north northwest as the Woods Trail. The Flume Trail continues straight to the northwest for another 0.2 mile before joining the Bemrose Creek Trail on the left. Your return on the Flume will take approximately the same length of time as your outward route because the trail is relatively flat. Back at the Hoosier Pass trailhead Mount Lincoln can be seen to the west southwest and Quandary Peak to the northwest.

Northern trailhead for Flume Trail at Hoosier Pass.   PHOTO BY DAVE MULLER

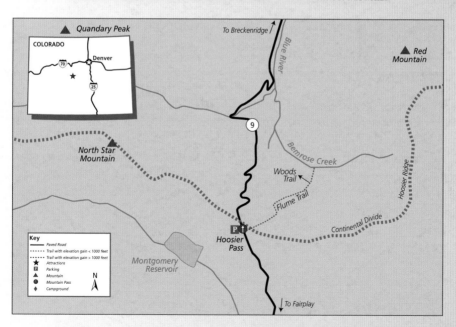

79. Francie's Cabin

HIKE DISTANCE	2.4 miles each way
TOUR TIME	Up in 70 minutes, down in 30 minutes
STARTING ELEVATION	10,380 feet
HIGHEST ELEVATION	11,264 feet
ELEVATION GAIN	896 feet (includes 6 extra feet each way)
DIFFICULTY	More difficult
AVALANCHE DANGERS	Least, but significantly higher above and beyond the hut
RELEVANT MAPS	Trails Illustrated Number 109 Breckenridge 7.5 minute Summit County Number Two Arapaho National Forest— Dillon Ranger District

GETTING THERE: From Ski Hill Road in Breckenridge, drive south on Colorado 9 for 2.1 miles and turn right onto Crown Drive. Follow Crown Drive for 0.5 mile and then turn right onto the Spruce Creek Road. Keep straight at all forks. After 1.1 miles, park near the Spruce Creek Trail sign. If your vehicle lacks the traction to reach this point, park off the road sooner.

COMMENT: Francie's Cabin, located south of the Breckenridge Ski Area, is named after Frances Lockwood Bailey and is part of the Summit County Huts and Trails Association. It can be rented through the Tenth Mountain Division Hut Association (970-925-5775). The huts are not open to non-renters. Please respect the privacy of those staying overnight at the cabin.

THE TOUR: From the parking area, begin southwest up the Spruce Creek Road. Keep left after 200 yards as the right fork rises more steeply toward Lower Crystal Lake. (You will join this route later just below Francie's Cabin.) After a 1.3-mile ascent, you will reach a clearing and a four-way intersection and some signs. The left fork leads to McCullough Gulch. Going straight leads to the Mohawk Lakes Trailhead. You will ascend to the right (north) toward the Wheeler Trail. In 75 yards you will pass around a barrier to vehicles and shortly thereafter a Wheeler Trail sign on the left. Ascend the wide road 0.8 mile further to a crossing of an upper segment of Crystal Creek. The road turns to the right and rises more steeply past the creek. Quickly pass another road barrier, and take the left fork up the steep road. (The steep route you passed at the first fork enters the road on the right just above this road barrier.) You now ascend into a clearing and follow the road as it again curves sharply to the right to reach Francie's Cabin just above some open slopes on your left. Take in the gorgeous surroundings before your initial steep descent and the gentler terrain further down the road.

Francie's Cabin was named for Frances Lockwood Bailey.

PHOTO BY DAVE MULLER

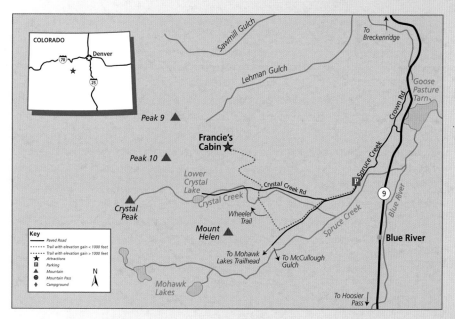

171

80. French Gulch

TOUR DISTANCE	3.1 miles each way
TOUR TIME	Up in 80 minutes, down in 55 minutes
STARTING ELEVATION	10,280 feet
HIGHEST ELEVATION	10,880 feet
ELEVATION GAIN	820 feet (includes 110 extra feet each way)
DIFFICULTY	Easiest
AVALANCHE DANGER	Moderate in the upper third portion of the tour
RELEVANT MAPS	Trails Illustrated Number 109 Boreas Pass 7.5 minute Summit County Number Two Arapaho National Forest—Dillon Ranger District

GETTING THERE: On Colorado 9, drive south from Main Street in Frisco for 8.5 miles and turn left onto Summit County Road 450. Follow County Road 450 and take the right fork at 0.3 miles. You will pass under a portal and through a housing development. At 1 mile from Colorado 9, go left onto Summit County Road 2 and continue past remnants of old mines and some new housing up into French Gulch. After 2.8 miles on Road 2, park on the right. Summit County maintains the road up to this point, which is 3.8 miles from Colorado 9.

COMMENT: The tour up French Gulch is popular and closed to snowmobiles. The route follows an old mining road, which gradually ascends to an open basin surrounded by several high peaks. There are a few private cabins off the trail along the way.

THE TOUR: From the parking area, head east along the wide road. Avoid the immediate left fork toward Humbug Hill and the right fork, which leads to the Barber Mine, 50 yards further. Continue up the gulch on the main road with the creek always on your right. Pass around a gate, and, after 1.3 miles from the trailhead, keep straight and avoid the two consecutive left forks. The second of these forks leads up Little French Gulch. Soon you will pass some open slopes above on your left. There is some avalanche risk, especially as the snow depth increases. You then enter a clearing with willows on your right. Beyond these is a large open area. The southern edge of the clearing, just before the trees, is the terminus of this ski tour. There are two options if you wish to go farther. The first is up to the southeast toward French Pass, and the second is to the right across the creek, south to a small slanted clearing, where some free skiing is possible. Your return down French Gulch offers the skier several gentle downhill runs.

Along the route in French Gulch.

PHOTO BY DAVE MULLER

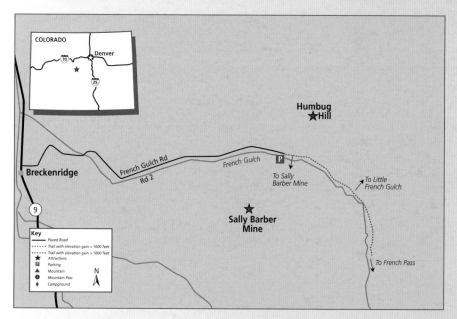

81. Gold Hill

TOUR DISTANCE	2.4 miles each way
TOUR TIME	Up in 100 minutes, down in 50 minutes (snowshoer's times)
STARTING ELEVATION	9,200 feet
HIGHEST ELEVATION	10,200 feet
ELEVATION	1,110 feet (includes 55 extra feet each way)
DIFFICULTY	More difficult
AVALANCHE DANGER	Least
RELEVANT MAPS	Trails Illustrated Number 108 Frisco 7.5 minute Summit County Number Two Arapaho National Forest— Dillon Ranger District

GETTING THERE: From the intersection with Main Street in Frisco, drive south on Colorado 9 for 4.9 miles and park on the right at the Gold Hill Trailhead.

THE COMMENT: The Gold Hill Trail uses part of the Colorado Trail and connects Colorado Highway 9 with the Peaks Trail to the west. The steep terrain makes this more of a snowshoe trail, but the expert cross-country skier might enjoy it as well. The trail is very well marked by blue diamonds, tree cuts (blazes), and occasional signage.

THE TOUR: Start on foot up the clear trail leading west. The trail rises steadily and arrives at a five-way intersection after 1 mile. Avoid side trails and follow the blue diamonds. Take the second left at this intersection. As you ascend through the forest, there are occasional great views of the area. At 2.4 miles, you come to a wooden Colorado Trail pole in a clearing with a great vista to the east. The mountains of the Tenmile Range peek up to the west. This is your turnaround point. (The trail continues upward another 0.5 mile before descending to the Miners Creek drainage and the Peaks Trail.) The return will delight the snowshoer and challenge the skier.

SIDEBAR: CAR KEYS

Here is a worthwhile habit to prevent you from losing your keys. When all the gear is out of the car, lock the door, hold the keys up in the air, and turn to one of your trustworthy companions and say, "keys." Place the keys in a pocket, zip or velcro the pocket closed, make eye contact with your companion, pat the pocket, and say "keys" again. This way you'll know that your keys are in the jacket you left at the first rest stop.

View from upper Gold Hill Trail.

PHOTO BY DAVE MULLER

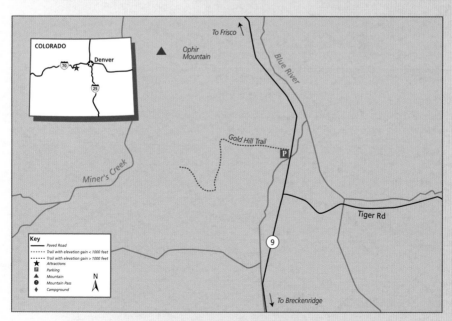

82. Hunkidori Mine

TOUR DISTANCE	3.6 miles each way
TOUR TIME	Up in 78 minutes, down in 68 minutes
STARTING ELEVATION	10,300 feet
HIGHEST ELEVATION	10,990 feet
ELEVATION GAIN	1,310 feet (includes 310 extra feet each way)
DIFFICULTY	More difficult
AVALANCHE DANGER	Moderate at the mine
RELEVANT MAPS	Trails Illustrated Number 104
	Montezuma 7.5 minute
	Keystone 7.5 minute
	Summit County Number Two
	Arapaho National Forest – Dillon Ranger District

GETTING THERE: Drive on U.S. 6, either 8.5 miles south from Loveland Pass or 7.8 miles east from Interstate 70 at Silverthorne (exit 205). Turn south onto the road to the Montezuma Road and follow it for 5.7 miles into the town of Montezuma.

WARNING: Since this book was first published in 2007, property owners near the trailhead have done everything in their power to limit access to this route by getting No Parking signs placed everywhere. This is a great route worth doing; have someone drop you off.

THE TOUR: Begin down the road to the south southwest. Cross the Snake River and ascend to the right. Keep straight after 0.2 mile as a road leads to the left. After an ascent of 0.5 mile from the trailhead, you will reach a fork. The left fork continues up to the former town of Saints John. You descend the right fork to the southwest. Leave potential snowmobile traffic and pass a mine remnant and an open area on your left. About 100 yards past the last fork, keep right at another fork and follow the trail as it rises and falls to the north and west to eventually reach Grizzly Gulch in a counterclockwise direction. The last mile becomes steeper. Shortly before your destination, you reach a fork with an abandoned truck partially buried on your left. The right fork leads quickly to two abandoned mining cabins. You ascend the left fork into a basin at the foot of the Hunkidori Mine. Beware of significant avalanche danger above and past the mine. Refresh yourself before the fast return.

SIDEBAR: SUNGLASSES

This isn't about making a fashion statement; this is about protecting your eyes from ultraviolet rays and glare. Buy sunglasses that filter 99% of UVA and UVB light. Buy them from a reputable firm. Wraparound sunglasses or sunglasses with side protection are a must.

The trail on the way to Hunkidori Mine.

PHOTO BY DAVE MULLER

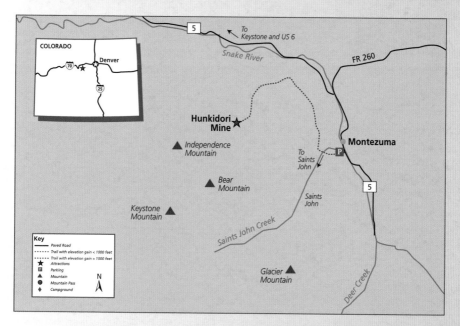

83. Keystone Gulch

TOUR DISTANCE	3.0 miles each way
TOUR TIME	Up in 94 minutes, down in 48 minutes
STARTING ELEVATION	9,265 feet
HIGHEST ELEVATION	10,230 feet
ELEVATION GAIN	989 feet (includes 12 extra feet each way)
DIFFICULTY	Easiest
AVALANCHE DANGER	Least
RELEVANT MAPS	Trails Illustrated Number 104 Keystone 7.5 minute Summit County Number Two Arapaho National Forest—Dillon Ranger District

GETTING THERE: From Interstate 70 at Silverthorne, take exit 205 and drive southeast on U.S. 6 for 5.5 miles. Turn right at the first stoplight into the Keystone Resort and keep left and then turn right onto Soda Ridge Road. Follow Soda Ridge Road for 0.4 mile and turn left onto the unpaved Keystone Gulch Road. Ascend this road for 0.1 mile and park on the left just before the open gate and Forest Service kiosk.

COMMENT: Ski touring or snowshoeing up the wide, gradual Keystone Gulch Road brings you to some of Keystone Ski Area's alpine ski lifts. This outing ends at the Santiago Lift, where there are food facilities, picnic tables, and toilets. The return is one continuous glide, with occasional double-poling.

THE TOUR: Begin on foot up the wide road to the southeast. Ascend gradually as the road snakes up the valley through the forest. Stay on the main road, which reaches several huts and lifts on the left at a junction, after 3 miles from the trailhead. The road continues up Keystone Gulch, but you ascend to the left. Here is where the views open up. Enjoy the amenities and the scenery before your pleasant return.

SIDEBAR: GARBAGE BAG

We carry a heavy-duty garbage bag in the bottom of our pack so that when we set our pack in snow, the contents don't get wet. The garbage bag can also be used as something to sit on in the snow, an improvised sled for a downhill run, or an extra layer of clothing in really bad weather. If you are going to use your garbage bag as an extra layer of clothing, may we suggest that beforehand you cut holes in the garbage bag for your head and arms.

Keystone Gulch Trailhead.

PHOTO BY DAVE MULLER

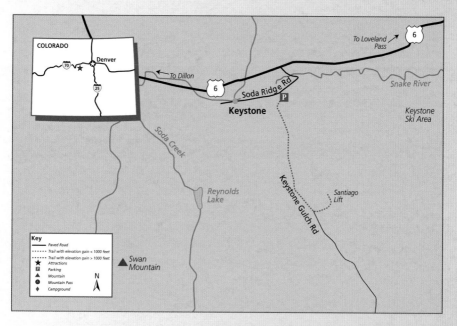

84. Lily Pad Lake via Ryan Gulch Road

TOUR DISTANCE	1.7 miles each way
TOUR TIME	Out in 40 minutes, back in 40 minutes
STARTING ELEVATION	9,800 feet
HIGHEST ELEVATION	9,900 feet
ELEVATION GAIN	755 feet (includes 655 extra feet)
DIFFICULTY	Easiest
AVALANCHE DANGER	Least
RELEVANT MAPS	Trails Illustrated Number 108
	Frisco 7.5 minute
	Summit County Number Two
	Arapaho National Forest—Dillon Ranger District

GETTING THERE: Take exit 205 from Interstate 70 and drive north on Colorado 9 for 0.2 mile. Then turn left on Wilderness Road (which becomes Ryan Gulch Road) and drive for 3.3 miles. Park on the left near the western edge of Ryan Gulch Road.

COMMENT: There are several routes to Lily Pad Lake. This one is quite popular. It begins from the Ryan Gulch Road and then passes along the lower slopes of Buffalo Mountain in the Eagles Nest Wilderness. The Wilderness rules exclude snowmobiles. The narrow trail winds mostly through the forest and is marked by tree blazes. There are few vistas until you reach the lake.

THE TOUR: Begin south up the blocked road to a high point before entering the woods on the clear trail, which rises and falls and soon passes a wilderness sign. After 1.4 miles from the trailhead, pass the Salt Lick Trail on the left. Continue to the right (southwest) and descend past a small pond on the left before reaching Lily Pad Lake. On a clear day, Peak One is visible to the south and Buffalo Mountain to the northwest. Return to the northwest by retracing your route back to the trailhead.

SIDEBAR: GEAR LISTS

There is little doubt that, at one time or another, we have all been accused of having way too much outdoor gear, particularly if we have left a pile of it in the foyer. And just as likely, we have arrived at a trailhead without an important piece of gear like a water bottle. The simple solution is to make a gear list of everything you need for a specific outdoor activity. Keep the list on your computer's hard drive, where you can print or revise it as needed.

Tony Bianchi at Lily Pad Lake.

PHOTO BY DAVE MULLER

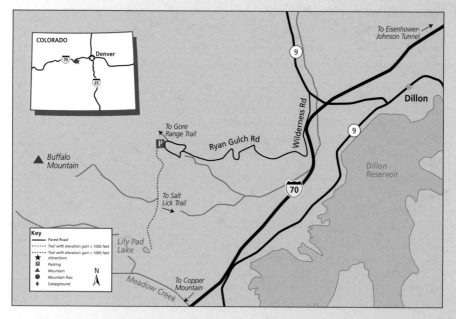

85. Lily Pad Lake via Salt Lick Trail

TOUR DISTANCE	3.1 miles each way
TOUR TIME	Up in 94 minutes, down in 56 minutes
STARTING ELEVATION	8,965 feet
HIGHEST ELEVATION	10,040 feet
ELEVATION GAIN	1,440 feet (includes 365 extra feet)
DIFFICULTY	More difficult
AVALANCHE DANGER	Least
RELEVANT MAPS	Trails Illustrated Number 108
	Frisco 7.5 minute
	Summit County Number Two
	Arapaho National Forest—Dillon Ranger District

GETTING THERE: From Colorado 9, in Silverthorne 100 yards north of Interstate 70 at Exit 205, turn west on Wildernest Road and set your mileage to zero. Drive up the Wildernest Road for 0.9 mile and turn left onto an unpaved road just before the Wildernest Road curves sharply to the right. Follow this side road for 0.1 mile and park near the trailhead signboard and road barrier. Regular cars can usually reach this parking area.

COMMENT: Of the three routes to Lily Pad Lake, north of Frisco in the Eagles Nest Wilderness, the most scenic goes by way of the Salt Lick Trail. The last half of this trek, however, becomes rather steep. Nordic skiers may require climbing skins, but snowshoers should be fine. Due to the relatively low elevation and considerable exposure to the sun, this outing should be best in February and early March when the snowpack is likely to be deeper.

THE TOUR: Start on foot up the road to the southwest around the metal barrier. After 150 yards, keep straight at the four-way intersection. For the first half of this tour, you will pass through several meadows. After 0.8 mile, you reach an important fork. As the road steepens and curves to the right, you leave the road on a trail on the left (southwest) and cross the creek before curving right and continuing up the valley. Cross open terrain until you reach a wilderness sign and some fencing. The trail will soon become steeper as you rise to a junction with the Lily Pad Trail at a sign at 2.6 miles of your tour. Continue to the left (southwest) for 0.5 mile and descend gradually before reaching the small Lily Pad Lake. Peak One can be seen to the south. The return is full of good ski gliding once you have reached the high point of the Salt Lick Trail.

TOP: Toward Salt Lick Trailhead.

PHOTOS BY DAVE MULLER

BOTTOM: Salt Lick Trailhead.

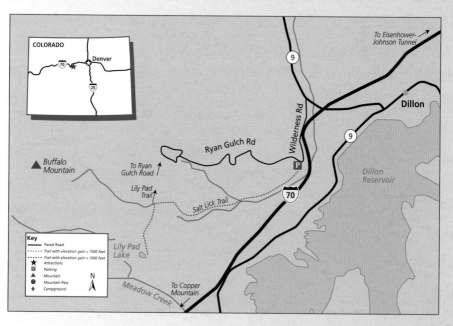

86. Little French Gulch

TOUR DISTANCE	2.6 miles each way
TOUR TIME	Up in 68 minutes, down in 35 minutes
STARTING ELEVATION	10,260 feet
HIGHEST ELEVATION	11,060 feet
ELEVATION GAIN	820 feet (includes 10 feet extra each way).
DIFFICULTY	More difficult
AVALANCHE DANGER	Least
RELEVANT MAPS	Trails Illustrated Number 109 Boreas Pass 7.5 minute Summit County Number Two Arapaho National Forest—Dillon Ranger District

GETTING THERE: From the traffic light at North Park Avenue on Colorado 9 in Breckenridge, drive south for 0.5 mile and turn left onto Wellington Road. Follow Wellington Road as it winds up into French Gulch. Keep right at mile 1.1 and park on the right at the end of county road maintenance. This point is 3.9 miles from Colorado 9.

COMMENT: French Gulch, northeast of Breckenridge, offers many ski and snowshoe touring possibilities. This route, to a cabin just below timberline, provides some exciting downhill runs on the descent. Mount Guyot looms above Little French Gulch to the southeast and, on your return, the peaks of the Tenmile Range are prominent to the west.

THE TOUR: Begin on a wide road southeast from the parking area. At 100 yards take the right fork and avoid the road up Humbug Hill. After another 50 yards, keep left at the fork and follow the main road east up the valley. Follow the gentle grade and bypass a private road on your left after 1.5 miles from the trailhead. After another 100 yards, take the left fork at the sign for Little French Gulch. The route becomes steeper as you ascend. Continue straight (east) at the four-way trail intersection. After 1 mile up the gulch, you reach your destination, a private cabin on your left. If you wish to continue higher in the gulch, you will probably have to break trail; beware of avalanche possibilities. Be prepared for your steep return to French Gulch.

SIDEBAR: POCKET KNIFE

Carry a pocket knife with two sharp blades, a can opener, a bottle opener, a hole punch, and corkscrew. At one time or another we have found all these tools useful, particularly the corkscrew.

A CMC group headed out of Little French Gulch to Mount Guyot.

PHOTO BY DAVID HITE

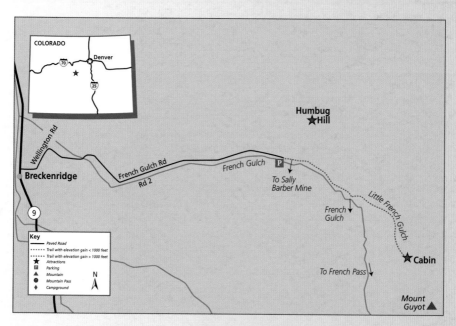

185

87. McCullough Gulch (lower)

TOUR DISTANCE	2.4 miles each way
TOUR TIME	Up in 79 minutes, down in 41 minutes
STARTING ELEVATION	10,300 feet
HIGHEST ELEVATION	11,140 feet
ELEVATION GAIN	1,070 feet (includes 115 extra feet each way)
DIFFICULTY	More difficult
AVALANCHE DANGER	Least
RELEVANT MAPS	Trails Illustrated Number 109 Breckenridge 7.5 minute Summit County Number Two Arapaho National Forest—Dillon Ranger District

GETTING THERE: From the southern edge of Breckenridge at the beginning of the Boreas Pass Road, drive south on Colorado 9 for 5.2 miles and park in the plowed area on the right.

COMMENT: Most winter recreationists use the upper road (Road 851) into McCullough Gulch. This other lower route, which will be described, avoids snowmobiles and proceeds directly up into the gulch on an old mining road. McCullough Gulch is bordered on the west by several of Colorado's highest peaks, and on a clear day the viewing can be special.

THE TOUR: From the parking area, take the trail that quickly leads north to the old mining road. Then go left and follow the road as it curves up into the forest and McCullough Gulch, with the drainage area on the left. Ascend gradually to the west and pass a cabin ruin at about 1 mile from the trailhead. Continue up the gulch and reach a T-intersection in an open area. An old mine is visible ahead and Quandary Peak looms above on the left. The Wheeler Trail rises to the right, but you descend to the left (south southwest), cross the creek, and then ascend to Road 851. Keep left when you reach this road, enjoy the scenery, and ascend 0.5 mile to the high point of this outing. This makes a good place to turn around for a faster descent back to your starting point.

SIDEBAR: TRAIL BLAZES

Different colored blazes mean different things in the National Parks, National Forests, and Bureau of Land Management trails. Sometimes trails are well marked with blazes that are hacks in the bark of trees, and sometimes the blazes are few and far between. Our only suggestion is to pay attention to the blazes and remember where you saw the last one. If, while breaking trail, you feel like you may be lost, backtrack to the last blaze and try again.

Quandary Peak from McCullough Gulch.

PHOTO BY DAVE MULLER

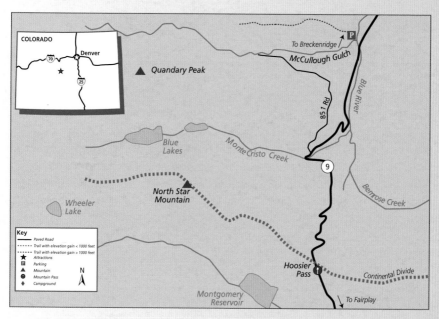

187

88. Mesa Cortina

TOUR DISTANCE	3.5 miles each way
TOUR TIME	Out in 105 minutes, back in 90 minutes
STARTING ELEVATION	9,220 feet
HIGHEST ELEVATION	9,700 feet
ELEVATION GAIN	1,010 feet (includes 530 extra feet)
DIFFICULTY	More difficult
AVALANCHE DANGER	Least
RELEVANT MAPS	Trails Illustrated Number 108 Frisco 7.5 minute Dillon 7.5 minute Willow Lakes 7.5 minute Summit County Number Two

GETTING THERE: From Interstate 70 at exit 205, drive north at Silverthorne for 200 yards and turn left on the Wildernest Road at the traffic light. After 0.2 mile from Colorado 9, turn right on Adams Avenue and then quickly turn left onto Buffalo Mountain Drive. At 1 mile from Colorado 9, turn right onto Lakeview Drive. After 0.4 mile more, turn left onto Aspen Drive. Look for the parking area on the right after another 150 yards.

COMMENT: The Mesa Cortina Trail traverses the eastern flanks of the Gore Range from a residential area to South Willow Creek, where it meets the Gore Range Trail. This demanding trail is not used by snowmobilers. It descends and rises several times before reaching a turnaround point at an open meadow below Buffalo Mountain, within the Eagles Nest Wilderness.

THE TOUR: Start to the north northwest from the trailhead signboard. Gradually descend to a clearing with good views of the Blue River Valley to the east. Enter the trees and reach another clearing before ascending a steep section in sparse forest. This second quarter of the Mesa Cortina Trail is the most demanding part for the cross-country skier. Using climbing skins for this segment both ways, whether sidestepping or walking, is a good idea. The snowshoer should have no trouble. Continue your undulating route, and keep left at two forks before reaching a narrow log bridge over South Willow Creek. Just beyond lies a signed intersection with the Gore Range Trail. Ascend the left (southwest) trail for another 0.7 mile to an open meadow, with Buffalo Mountain towering impressively above. This is a good terminus, as the trail continues more steeply up to the west, with no clear destination prior to Red Buffalo or Eccles Passes. The return is about as difficult as your outbound route.

D.J. Inman, Tony Bianchi, and Chris Belle at Mesa Cortina
terminus below Buffalo Mountain.

PHOTO BY DAVE MULLER

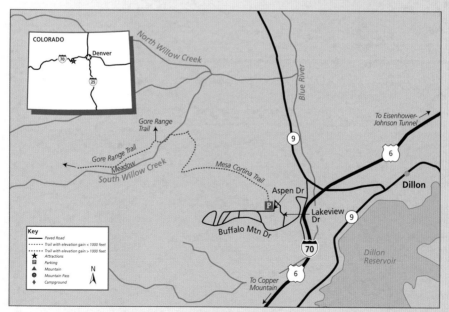

189

89. North Rock Creek Trail

TOUR DISTANCE	2.7 miles each way
TOUR TIME	Up in 64 minutes, down in 45 minutes
STARTING ELEVATION	8,830 feet
HIGHEST ELEVATION	9,620 feet
ELEVATION GAIN	1,040 feet (includes 250 extra feet)
DIFFICULTY	Easiest
AVALANCHE DANGER	Least
RELEVANT MAPS	Trails Illustrated Number 108 Willow Lakes 7.5 minute Summit County Numbers One and Two Arapaho National Forest—Dillon Ranger District

GETTING THERE: From exit 205 on Interstate 70, drive north on Colorado 9 for 7.7 miles and turn left onto the Rock Creek Road. (This turnoff is opposite the Blue River Campground.) Drive up Rock Creek Road for 1.3 miles. Turn left and go another 30 yards to the skier parking sign and park.

COMMENT: North Rock Creek lies in a little-used area in the Eagles Nest Wilderness east of Keller Mountain and north of Silverthorne off of Colorado 9. The route begins on a wide road and then continues on a trail to an abandoned cinder-block cabin ruin at the far edge of a vast, flat meadow.

THE TOUR: Start south up the road, which rises and falls as it curls up the valley through evergreen forest for 1.4 miles to the summer Rock Creek Trailhead and parking area. On your way to this trailhead, avoid any side trails on the left and remain on the main wide road. North Rock Creek will always be on your left. At the Rock Creek Trailhead sign, keep to the left and quickly ascend the trail past a register, a signboard, and a sign indicating that you are entering the Alfred M. Bailey Bird Nesting Area. At 0.5 mile past the Rock Creek Trailhead, cross the Gore Range Trail and continue straight (south) up the gradual trail. In less than another 1 mile, descend to the left at a fork as the main trail continues straight and eventually ends higher up at the old Boss Mine. This left fork takes you around some fallen timber before the trail curves to the right and skirts the edge of a large clearing leading directly to a ruined hut. This is the terminus of this outing. Keller Mountain looms above to the west southwest, and Williams Peak may be visible to the northeast across the meadow. The return will provide the skier with several pleasant downhill runs.

A snowshoer breaks trail along the North Rock Creek Trail.

PHOTO BY TERRY ROOT

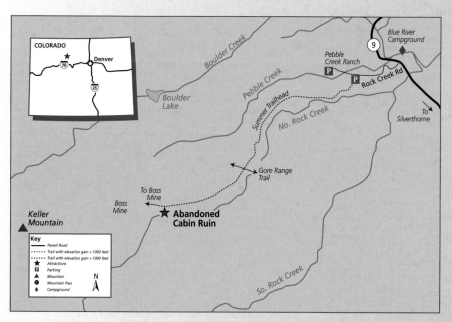

90. North Tenmile Creek

TOUR DISTANCE	3.5 miles each way
HIKING TIME	Up in 110 minutes, down in 88 minutes
STARTING ELEVATION	9,150 feet
HIGHEST ELEVATION	10,070 feet
ELEVATION GAIN	1,540 feet (includes 310 extra feet each way)
DIFFICULTY	More difficult
RELEVANT MAPS	Trails Illustrated Number 108 Frisco 7.5 minute Vail Pass 7.5 minute Summit County Number Two

GETTING THERE: From Interstate 70 take exit 201 (Frisco). Park on the north side of the highway and access roads at the road barrier.

COMMENT: The North Tenmile Creek Trail leads into the Eagles Nest Wilderness with the creek always on the left. After 3.5 miles through forest and meadow, it reaches a junction with the Gore Range Trail. This will be the turnaround point for this tour.

THE TOUR: Start out to the west from the road barrier and quickly take two right forks. Because of the steep trail, the skier may wish to walk up this initial segment. Blue diamond markers on the trees clarify the route. After almost 2 miles, enter the Eagles Nest Wilderness at a sign in a meadow. Continue the next 1.6 miles to a junction with the Gore Range Trail. The left fork rises to Uneva Pass, and the trail on the right leads to Eccles Pass. Return by your ascent route.

SIDEBAR: WINDCHILL CHART

		TEMPERATURE															
	CALM	40	35	30	25	20	15	10	5	0	−5	−10	−15	−20	−25	−30	−35
	5	36	31	25	19	13	7	1	−5	−11	−16	−22	−28	−34	−40	−46	−52
W	10	34	27	21	15	9	3	−4	−10	−16	−22	−28	−35	−41	−47	−53	−59
I	15	32	25	19	13	6	0	−7	−13	−19	−26	−32	−39	−45	−51	−58	−64
N	20	30	24	17	11	4	−2	−9	−15	−22	−29	−35	−42	−48	−55	−61	−68
D	25	29	23	16	9	3	−4	−11	−17	−24	−31	−37	−44	−51	−58	−64	−71
	30	28	22	15	8	1	−5	−12	−19	−26	−33	−39	−46	−53	−60	−67	−73
	35	28	21	14	7	0	−7	−14	−21	−27	−34	−41	−48	−55	−62	−69	−76
	40	27	20	13	6	−1	−8	−15	−22	−29	−36	−43	−50	−57	−64	−71	−78
	45	26	19	12	5	−2	−9	−16	−23	−30	−37	−44	−51	−58	−65	−72	−79
	50	26	19	12	4	−3	−10	−17	−24	−31	−38	−45	−52	−60	−67	−74	−81

Linda Grey and Tua at the North Tenmile Creek Trailhead. PHOTO BY TERRY ROOT

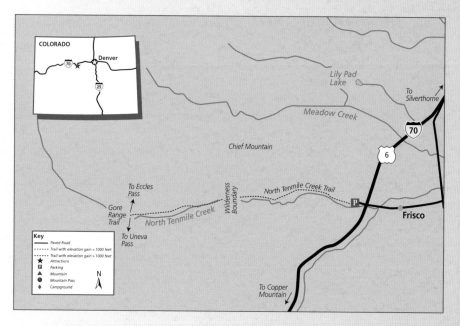

193

91. Peaks Trail – Breckenridge to Frisco

TOUR DISTANCE	8.5 miles one way
TOUR TIME	Down in 170 minutes
STARTING ELEVATION	10,030 feet
HIGHEST ELEVATION	10,240 feet
LOWEST ELEVATION	9,100 feet
ELEVATION GAIN	995 feet (includes 785 extra feet one way)
DIFFICULTY	More difficult
AVALANCHE DANGER	Least
RELEVANT MAPS	Trails Illustrated Numbers 109 and 108 Frisco 7.5 minute Summit County Number Two Arapaho National Forest – Dillon Ranger District

GETTING THERE: This full tour requires transportation to each end. For the Frisco trailhead, beginning from the intersection of Main Street and Colorado 9 in Frisco, drive south on Colorado 9 for 0.5 mile and turn right. After 75 yards, turn right again and make a quick left turn onto a road that leads directly to the trailhead in 200 yards. For the Breckenridge trailhead, drive on Colorado 9 to Breckenridge, turn west onto Ski Hill Road, and set your odometer to zero. Drive on Ski Hill Road for 2.3 miles and park on the left just past the trailhead signs on the left.

COMMENT: The Peaks Trail from Breckenridge to Frisco is one of my favorites. With the Tenmile Range above on your left, the route rises and falls while crossing the three Barton Creeks in its first half.

THE TOUR: From the Breckenridge trailhead go west northwest. Blue diamond tree blazes mark the trail. Go 0.9 mile and continue straight at the four-way trail intersection at Cucumber Creek. Over the next 2.5 miles you will cross South, Middle, and North Barton Creeks. Less than 75 yards beyond North Barton Creek, the trail forks left (northwest) at a sign. Another 0.4 mile brings you to a large clearing, which slopes to the east. Ascend the middle of the clearing to the northwest past a solitary pole at the middle of this meadow. You are now a little further than halfway to Frisco. The trail will offer steeper downhill runs for the next few miles. After 1 mile north of the large clearing, continue straight at the trail junction with the Colorado Trail and the Miners Creek Trail to the left. Pass the Gold Hill Trail on the right 0.7 mile further. There will be 2 miles of creek crossings and steep downhill sections before you reach the Miners Creek Road near Rainbow Lake. Follow the road down to the right, and curve left after 0.4 mile. Descend to the summer bicycle path. Then take the second trail on the left at the five-way intersection and descend the final 200 yards to your vehicle at the Frisco end of your trek.

TOP: Breckenridge Trailhead for Peaks Trail.   PHOTO BY DAVE MULLER

BOTTOM: Trailhead sign.   PHOTO BY DAVID HITE

195

92. Pennsylvania Creek

TOUR DISTANCE	4.2 miles each way
TOUR TIME	Up in 112 minutes, down in 84 minutes
STARTING ELEVATION	10,320 feet
HIGHEST ELEVATION	11,740 feet
ELEVATION GAIN	1,980 feet (includes 280 extra feet each way)
DIFFICULTY	More difficult
AVALANCHE DANGER	Moderate at higher elevations
RELEVANT MAPS	Trails Illustrated Number 109 Boreas Pass 7.5 minute Breckenridge 7.5 minute Summit County Number Two

GETTING THERE: From Ski Hill Road in Breckenridge, drive south on Colorado 9 for 4.2 miles. Turn left onto the Blue River Road and set your mileage to zero. Avoid three consecutive roads on the right before turning right onto Royal Drive at 0.2 mile from Colorado 9. Ascend Royal Drive and keep right after 80 yards. You are now on Regal Circle. At 0.5 mile from Colorado 9, turn right onto Coronet Road. After 0.2 mile, continue straight at the four-way intersection. Keep left after another 0.1 mile as Holly Lane leads to the right. Stay on this main road for another 0.4 mile and park as the plowed road ends.

COMMENT: Besides the complex route to the trailhead, the route up Pennsylvania Creek adds steepness and considerable elevation gain as further challenges. The rewards are a very beautiful outing to a picturesque basin below the Continental Divide. Climbing skins are recommended for the skier for much of the ascent to timberline.

THE TOUR: From the road end, begin northwest up a straight trail. Avoid the trail on the right within 50 yards. (This steep trail will connect with your route.) After another 50 yards, the trail curves right (southeast) and becomes very steep for 0.3 mile before rising more moderately up the valley with Pennsylvania Creek on the right. Keep left at two trail junctions and rise to a crossing of Pennsylvania Creek at mile 2.6 of your trek. After another steep segment, the trail becomes more level and the basin more spectacular. Keep the creek to your left and ascend parallel to it for the final steep third of this tour into Horseshoe Basin at timberline. You may have to make your own trail for the final 0.8 mile. Red Mountain lies to the west southwest at the head of the valley, and more imposing Red Peak lies to the southeast on the left. Stay at the lower end of the basin to minimize avalanche risk. The peaks of the Tenmile Range are to the west.

Red Peak at the headwaters of Pennsylvania Creek.

PHOTO BY DAVE COOPER

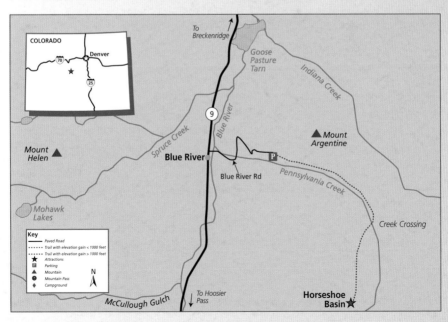

197

93. Rainbow Lake

TOUR DISTANCE	1.5 miles each way
TOUR TIME	Up in 42 minutes, down in 42 minutes
STARTING ELEVATION	9,100 feet
HIGHEST ELEVATION	9,270 feet
ELEVATION GAIN	254 (includes 42 extra feet each way)
DIFFICULTY	More difficult
AVALANCHE DANGER	Least
RELEVANT MAPS	Trails Illustrated Number 108
	Frisco 7.5 minute
	Summit County Number Two
	Arapaho National Forest – Dillon Ranger District

GETTING THERE: From Interstate 70 at Frisco, take exit 201. After 0.3 miles, park on the right in the large lot at the trailhead south of I-70.

COMMENT: The route to Rainbow Lake, outside of Frisco, is free of snowmobiles. It starts on the summer bike path and then enters the forest up to the lake. Blue diamond tree markers indicate the trail. Although there is only a modest elevation gain, there are a few steep sections. Beyond Rainbow Lake, the trail joins the Miners Creek Trail and the Peaks Trail. Rainbow Lake connects with Miners Creek, which flows into Dillon Reservoir.

THE TOUR: Begin to the east southeast from the parking area and cross Tenmile Creek. When you reach the summer bike path, follow it to the left. After 300 yards, pass the Mount Royal Trail on the right. At about 0.8 mile from the trailhead, you reach a four-way intersection and several signs. Leave the bike path here, descend slightly to the southeast, and quickly pass a signboard. Follow the trail across an open area before entering the trees. Continue straight at two four-way intersections, and then ascend to Rainbow Lake. The trail continues around the right margin of the lake. From Rainbow Lake, Buffalo Mountain is visible to the northwest; above to the southwest lie Tenmile Peak and Peak One. Be careful on the initial descent from the lake as you return.

SIDEBAR: DUCT TAPE

The Mountaineers neglected one very important item in their list of the Ten Essentials: duct tape. We recommend that you put a roll in a plastic bag that you toss into the bottom of your pack. It will come in handy when you need to do a field repair to your equipment or body. We have all seen the silver grey tape as a patch on a ripped or burned down jacket, but do you know that duct tape is great for covering a hot spot created by friction in your boot?

Peak One over Rainbow Lake.

PHOTO BY DAVE MULLER

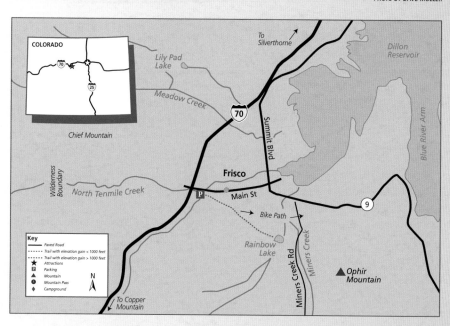

199

94. Saints John and Wild Irishman Mine

TOUR DISTANCE	2.8 miles each way
TOUR TIME	Up in 95 minutes, down in 45 minutes
STARTING ELEVATION	10,300 feet
HIGHEST ELEVATION	11,640 feet
ELEVATION GAIN	1,620 feet (includes 140 extra feet each way)
DIFFICULTY	More difficult
AVALANCHE DANGER	Moderate in the upper fifth of the tour
RELEVANT MAPS	Trails Illustrated Number 104
	Montezuma 7.5 minute
	Keystone 7.5 minute
	Summit County Number Two
	Arapaho National Forest – Dillon Ranger District

GETTING THERE: From exit 205 of Interstate 70 (the Dillon-Silverthorne exit), drive east on U.S. 6 for 7.5 miles. Just past the entrance into the Keystone Ski Area, turn right onto the Montezuma Road and set your mileage to zero. Drive up the wide, well-plowed Montezuma Road for 5.4 miles.

WARNING: Since this book was first published in 2007, property owners near the trailhead have done everything in their power to limit access to this route by getting No Parking signs placed everywhere. This is a great route worth doing; have someone drop you off.

THE TOUR: Begin down to the south southwest on the wide road and then ascend steeply as the road curves to the right. Avoid a side road on the left 200 yards from the trailhead. Follow two switchbacks up the main road before reaching a level area and a fork at the mouth of the valley. Keep left (south) as the right fork leads to the former Hunkidori Mine. Ascend more gradually and reach the town of Saints John at mile 1.3 of your tour. The road before the town can be icy at times. After passing extensive mine ruins on the left, the road turns sharply to the right at a junction, crosses Saints John Creek, and then curves sharply left beneath a cabin. Follow this road to the south. Higher in the basin, you pass through a fence with a signboard on the right. Continue up the open and very scenic valley to a fork at mile 2.3 of the tour. Descend here to the left (south southeast) and cross Saints John Creek again before a final steep 0.5 mile to two cabin ruins to the left of the road around the site of the former Wild Irishman Mine. Another 75 yards up the road leads to a lovely overlook of the Saints John Creek basin and beyond. Be careful on your steep return.

Linda Grey in front of a cabin near Saints John.

PHOTO BY TERRY ROOT

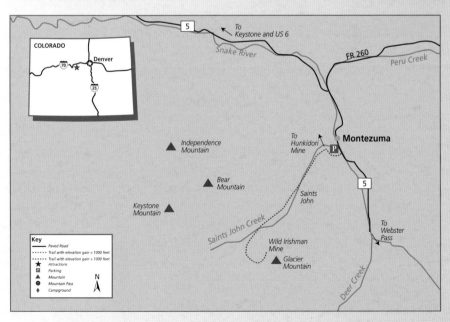

95. Sally Barber Mine

TOUR DISTANCE	1.4 miles each way
TOUR TIME	Up in 35 minutes, down in 24 minutes
STARTING ELEVATION	10,280 feet
HIGHEST ELEVATION	10,685 feet
ELEVATION GAIN	449 feet (includes 22 extra feet each way)
DIFFICULTY	Easiest
AVALANCHE DANGER	Least
RELEVANT MAP	Trails Illustrated Number 109 Boreas Pass 7.5 minute Summit County Number Two Arapaho National Forest—Dillon Ranger District

GETTING THERE: Drive 0.4 mile south on Colorado 9 from North Park Avenue in Breckenridge. Turn left on Wellington Road and continue for 3.9 miles. Park on the right at the end of county maintenance. En route to the parking area keep right at 1.1 miles.

COMMENT: The remnants of the Sally Barber Mine can be reached from the north or the south. The northern approach will be described. Historical signs at the mine tell some of the mine's history. Zinc was mined here between 1882 and 1920.

THE TOUR: Begin to the east up the wide road. After 100 yards, descend the right fork and cross the creek before the gradual ascent to the mine. At the ruins of the mine, there is a good overlook to the north. The road continues past the mine and down into Australia Gulch. The skier will enjoy the gentle downhill gliding on the return.

SIDEBAR: ALTITUDE SICKNESS

Three types of altitude sickness should be recognizable by skiers and snowshoers going into the backcountry: acute mountain sickness (AMS), high altitude pulmonary edema (HAPE), and high altitude cerebral edema (HACE). AMS makes you feel awful, but HAPE and HACE can kill you. What is truly odd about altitude sickness is that different people can be affected at different altitudes on different days. In other words, an onset of altitude sickness can happen to a flatlander and an experienced snowshoer at the same altitude. AMS symptoms include headache, loss of appetite, nausea, fatigue, dizziness, and insomnia. As your body acclimates to the change in altitude, these symptoms subside. HAPE and HACE are caused by fluids accumulating in the body.

Artifacts at Sally Barber Mine.

PHOTO BY DAVE MULLER

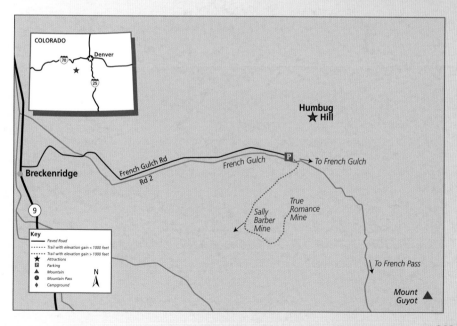

203

96. Spruce Creek Trail to Mohawk Lakes Trailhead

TOUR DISTANCE	2.8 miles each way
TOUR TIME	Up in 78 minutes, down in 52 minutes
STARTING ELEVATION	9,930 feet
HIGHEST ELEVATION	11,080 feet
ELEVATION GAIN	1,382 feet (includes 116 extra feet each way)
DIFFICULTY	More difficult
AVALANCHE DANGER	Least
RELEVANT MAPS	Trail Illustrated Number 109 Breckenridge 7.5 minute Summit County Number Two Arapaho National Forest—Dillon Ranger District

GETTING THERE: From South Park Avenue in Breckenridge, drive south on Colorado 9 for 2.4 miles. Turn right at the stop sign on the Spruce Creek Road, After 0.1 mile, follow the Spruce Creek Road as it curves left and continues another 1.1 miles to a parking area at the end of the plowed road. The Spruce Creek Trailhead is on the left at a sign.

COMMENT: The Spruce Creek Trail parallels the Spruce Creek Road south of Breckenridge and is often overlooked by snowshoers and cross-country skiers who use the road. This steep and demanding trail poses little difficulty for the snowshoer, but the skier will need good skills and probably skins to navigate the winding, narrow trail. The Spruce Creek Trail is marked by trail blazes. The trail runs mostly through the forest and receives little sun exposure. Therefore, be prepared for cold temperatures. Good views exist at only a few trail points and at the high point, the Mohawk Lakes trailhead.

THE TOUR: Begin on foot to the southeast into the forest. The early steep descent is indicative of the entire trail. Continue up through the trees and follow the tree cuts (blazes) that mark the trail. After almost 1 mile, cross Spruce Creek at a sign in a clearing. At 1.8 miles you reach a four-way intersection and sign just before a large open area. The Wheeler Trail passes to the left and to the right. Continue straight (south southwest) along the left side of the clearing, and ascend 1 mile to the end of the trail at a sign as it meets a road, some water facilities, and the Mohawk Lakes Trailhead nearby at the end of the road. Mount Helen looms above to the west. Return as you ascended or, for variety, descend onto the Spruce Creek Road, which will also take you back to the trailhead.

TOP: Mount Helen from Spruce Creek Trail.

PHOTOS BY DAVE MULLER

BOTTOM: Spruce Creek Trailhead.

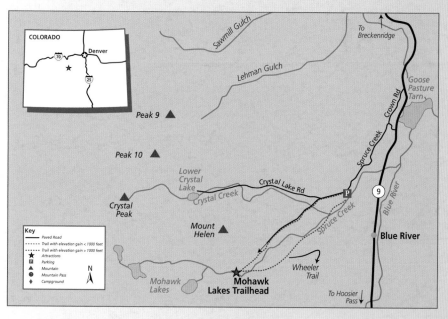

97. Spruce Creek Loop

TOUR DISTANCE	3.4 miles (total loop)
TOUR TIME	Up in 70 minutes, and down in 22 minutes
STARTING ELEVATION	9,930 feet
HIGHEST ELEVATION	10,940 feet
ELEVATION GAIN	1,155 feet (includes 145 extra feet)
DIFFICULTY	Most difficult
AVALANCHE DANGER	Least
RELEVANT MAPS	Trails Illustrated Number 109 Breckenridge 7.5 minute Summit County Number Two Arapaho National Forest—Dillon Ranger District

GETTING THERE: From South Park Avenue in Breckenridge, drive south on Colorado 9 for 2.4 miles. Turn right at the stop sign on the Spruce Creek Road. After 0.1 mile, follow the Spruce Creek Road as it curves to the left and continues another 1.1 miles to a parking area at the end of the plowed road.

COMMENT: The Spruce Creek Trail parallels the Spruce Creek Road and is often overlooked by winter recreationists. This steep and demanding route will pose little difficulty for the snowshoer, but the skier will likely need climbing skins to ascend the steep, winding, and narrow trail. Ascending Spruce Creek Trail, taking the Wheeler Trail over to the Spruce Creek Road, and then rapidly returning to your starting point at the parking area completes this clockwise loop. There are several stopping places along the way with great views of the surrounding peaks. There is no snowmobile traffic on the Spruce Creek Trail and very little such traffic on the lower part of the Spruce Creek Road.

THE TOUR: Begin to the southeast into the forest. An early steep descent is an indicator of what will follow. Continue up through the trees and follow the tree cuts (blazes), which mark the trail. After almost 1 mile, cross Spruce Creek at a sign. At mile 1.8, a four-way intersection and another sign are reached. The Wheeler Trail leads to the left and the right. The Spruce Creek Trail continues straight and will end at the Mohawk Lakes Trailhead. To continue this loop tour, take the Wheeler Trail on the right (west) and follow it up to the Spruce Creek Road at a four-way intersection. From here, descend northeast on the wide road for a rapid return to the parking area and your starting point.

Spruce Creek Loop and Mount Helen.

PHOTO BY DAVE MULLER

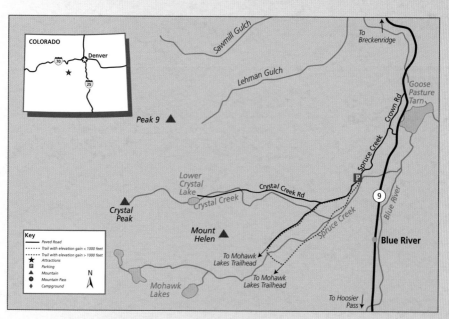

98. True Romance Mine

TOUR DISTANCE	2.2 miles each way
TOUR TIME	Up in 64 minutes, down in 40 minutes
STARTING ELEVATION	10,417 feet
HIGHEST ELEVATION	11,000 feet
ELEVATION GAIN	773 feet (includes 190 extra feet)
DIFFICULTY	Most difficult
AVALANCHE DANGER	Least
RELEVANT MAPS	Trails illustrated Number 109 Breckenridge 7.5 minute Boreas Pass 7.5 minute Summit County Number Two

GETTING THERE: From Colorado 9 at the southern edge of Breckenridge, drive up the Boreas Pass Road. Turn left on the Baldy Road for 0.9 mile. Then turn left on the Sally Barber Road for 0.2 mile and park on the side of the road at the trailhead.

COMMENT: The Breckenridge area is covered with the remains of old mines. This tour takes you to two of them. The Sally Barber Mine can also be reached from the east via French Gulch. Its remnants are impressive. On the other hand, The True Romance Mine has little visual impact. Both mine sites offer good views to the north and east. This area is honeycombed with unofficial side trails. Staying on the described route is recommended.

THE TOUR: Begin to the north northeast past a private paved road sign called Alphabet Road. Follow the level main trail until you pass under power lines at mile 1.2 of this tour. The trail then rises steeply before curving left and passing an old cabin on the left on your final ascent to the Sally Barber Mine. Signs at the mine site describe it. Enjoy this view before continuing up to the right (southeast). This very steep segment leads to a trail junction. Proceed to the left (north) on a fairly level trail through the trees and reach an old mine on the right and a wooden sign on the left at the True Romance Mine. This overlook is a good turnaround point. Return by your ascent route and be careful on the short, steep downhill segment above Sally Barber Mine.

SIDEBAR: SUNSCREEN

Use a sunscreen with an SPF of 15 or higher in the backcountry. We like the clear liquids that are just sunscreen and the waxy stuff that comes in what looks like a shoe polish can. Sunny days occur at least 300 days a year in Colorado. The Colorado mountains expose you to more ultraviolet rays than do the flatlands. So slap on the sunscreen.

D.J. Inman at the True Romance Mine.

PHOTO BY DAVE MULLER

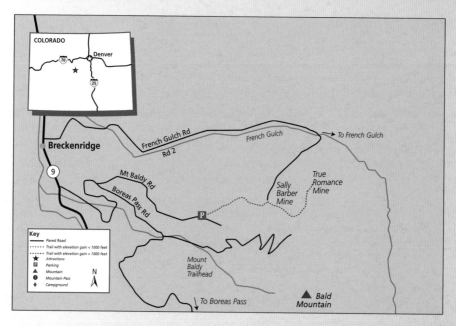

209

99. Tenmile Creek

TOUR DISTANCE	5.1 miles
TOUR TIMES	Up in 155 minutes, down in 107 minutes
STARTING ELEVATION	9,677 feet
HIGHEST ELEVATION	10,360 feet
ELEVATION GAIN	953 feet (includes 135 extra feet each way)
DIFFICULTY	More difficult
AVALANCHE DANGER	Least
RELEVANT MAPS	Trails Illustrated Number 108 and 109
	Vail Pass 7.5 minute
	Copper Mountain 7.5 minute
	Summit County Number Two

GETTING THERE: From Interstate 70 at Copper Mountain, take exit 195 onto Colorado 91. Quickly turn left onto the frontage road off the east side of Colorado 91. Drive 0.3 mile on this road, past a gas station, to the road's end. Park at the trailhead.

COMMENT: The Tenmile Trail takes the cross-country skier and the snowshoer through a lovely valley surrounded by towering peaks. The Tenmile Range lies on the left and ahead while the Copper Mountain Ski Area and Vail Pass lie to the right. This tour passes through Wheeler Flats, which is full of Gold Rush history. More than 10,000 people lived in this area in the last decades of the nineteenth century.

THE TOUR: Begin on foot to the north and cross a bridge over Tenmile Creek. Then turn right and continue south on the wide trail with Tenmile Creek on your right. Cross the scenic amphitheatre of Wheeler Flats until you reach a four-way intersection about 1 mile from the trailhead. A bridge on the right leads to Colorado 91, and the Wheeler Trail ascends to the left. You continue straight and cross an occasional small creek; The creeks should be frozen by January; however you may have to side step or remove your skis to cross some of them. An abandoned cabin lies on the right at mile 2.4 of your trek. Continue generally south and pass under several sets of power lines. The trail gently rises to reach an overlook point 40 yards from Colorado 91 at mile 5.1. This is your turnaround point.

SIDEBAR: MATCHES

Go buy some kitchen matches that you can strike on any surface. Buy a plastic bottle with a screw-on top. Put the matches in the bottle with a small strip of the striker material from the side of the box. Go to a smoke shop and buy a cigar lighter that you have to switch on to ignite. Toss the matches and lighter into the bottom of your pack and forget them.

D.J. Inman at Tenmile Creek trailhead.

PHOTO BY DAVE MULLER

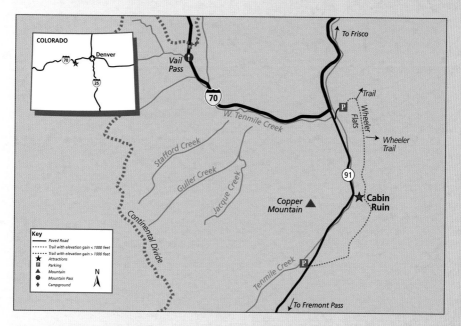

211

Further Reading

Apt, Alan. *Snowshoe Routes: Colorado's Front Range*. Seattle, Washington: Mountaineers Books, 2001.

Carr, Deborah and Landrigan, Lou. *Backcountry Skiing and Snowshoeing in Grand County, Colorado*. Tabernash, Colorado: Backcountry Bound, 2003.

DuMais, Richard. *50 Colorado Ski Tours*. Boulder, Colorado: High Peak Publishing, 1982.

Lightbody, Tari and Lightbody, Andy. *Winter Trails*. Old Saybrook, Connecticut: Globe Pequot Press, 1999.

Litz, Brian and Lankford, Kurt. *Skiing Colorado's Backcountry*. Golden, Colorado: Fulcrum Publishing, 1989.

Ohlrich, Warren H. *Crosscountry Skiing and Snowshoeing – Aspen and the Roaring Fork Valley*. Basalt, Colorado: Who Press, 1998.

Sudduth, Tom and Sudduth, Janse. *Central Colorado Ski Tours*. Boulder, Colorado: Pruett Publishing Company, 1977.

Walter, Claire. *Showshoeing Colorado*. Golden, Colorado: Fulcrum Publishing, 2003.

Index